Audacity

How to Make Decisions Quickly and Efficiently

Dan Desmarques

22 Lions

Audacity: How to Make Decisions Quickly and Efficiently

Written by Dan Desmarques

Contents

Introduction

In a world where uncertainty and indecision often paralyze us, the ability to make decisions quickly and effectively is a critical skill. "Audacity: How to Make Decisions Quickly and Efficiently" is a comprehensive guide designed to give you the tools and insights you need to navigate life's complexities with confidence. More than just a collection of theories, this book serves as a practical manual that draws on the author's extensive experience and wisdom to help you transform your decision-making process and achieve your goals.

What you will learn:

- Understand fear and indecision: Discover the root causes of fear and indecision and learn how to overcome them.

- The Art of Decision Making: Explore the elements that influence our decisions and how to think effectively to maximize results.

- Transformative Insights: Gain a deeper understanding of yourself and the role of wisdom in making the right choices.

- Practical Strategies: Learn actionable steps to make decisions quickly and efficiently, even in challenging situations.

- Real-Life Examples: Benefit from the author's personal experiences and anecdotes that illustrate the principles discussed.

Whether you are a student, a professional, or someone seeking personal growth, Audacity offers valuable insights and practical advice that can be applied to various aspects of your life. By understanding the dynamics of decision making and the factors that influence our choices, you can improve your ability to make informed and effective decisions. Don't let fear and indecision hold you back. " Audacity: How to Make Decisions Quickly and Efficiently" is your roadmap to confident and effective decision-making.

Chapter 1: The Challenge of Decision Making

Many of life's problems stem from the difficulty of making decisions or the fear of making the wrong ones. However, the experience of making mistakes and the constant fear of making mistakes do not necessarily improve our decision-making abilities. The right decision, made with confidence, comes from solid inner knowledge and is based on wisdom. While we may never have control over future realities, we can still make choices that increase our potential for success. Great leaders throughout history, as well as successful entrepreneurs, have often made the right decisions more often than others because they recognize elements of reality that many cannot see. We can learn to recognize these elements and think effectively to maximize our results in all situations.

Throughout our lives, we encounter problems to solve and dilemmas that require us to consider the best course of action. Ultimately, it is the outcome of our choices that reveals their significance. We cannot turn back time, and if we could, we might not have ventured so far in the wrong direction. But without those mistakes, we would not have learned. We constantly pursue truth without ever fully grasping it, because the truth we seek also transforms us. In the face of these transformations, we may lose many of the people we love and respect, as they are immersed in other realities with different challenges from our own.

The faster we learn and transform, the faster the process I have described will unfold. This does not mean, however, that our results will be more visible. Inner transformations are rarely visible to others. Only we understand the meaning of our sorrows, depressions, and fears. Others cannot understand these emotions in the same way because their souls have gone through different processes in other lives and places. We encounter many souls throughout our lives, all seeking the same happiness, peace, and spiritual fulfillment, but each pursuing it differently in different lives. If this were not the case, if the truth were already within us, all dilemmas would be mere illusions. In a sense, this is true if we look at problems as illusions of different levels:

First level: We face the power of inequality and unhappiness.

Second level: We face the polarity of choice and possibility.

Third level: We take responsibility for creating our problems.

At this final level, a person no longer says, "I was betrayed," but rather, "I chose the wrong person". They no longer say, "I was unemployed because I was fired," but rather, "I chose my job and the wrong path in life". They no longer say, "I am unhappy," but rather, "I must take responsibility for my own happiness".

Most people remain between the first and second stages, either because they choose to be slaves to money and the need to belong to a system that assigns them a social level, or because they feel dependent on emotional structures for survival. In addition, the vast majority of people live in fear of loneliness, which prevents them from exploring new paths in life. This fear manifests itself in various forms, such as the disapproval of others, criticism, and different ways of thinking that lead to social segregation.

For example, I have moved around a lot in my life, holding different jobs in different countries. As a result, everyone I met distanced themselves from me. They felt that the person they once knew was no longer the same person. This is quite normal because most people, although they have eyes to see, are blind to the soul of another person and the immortality of such a soul. People cling to stereotypes and superficial perceptions of reality. When these change, they feel as if the person has died and treat him as if he had died. So a person with many friends has nothing to be proud of; they haven't changed enough to lose them. But all this comes with the death of the body anyway.

When we learn to make the right choices, not those driven by our fears, all illusions fade and we take responsibility for our future. When that moment comes, we realize that "all beings in the world are in deep ignorance due to the illusion of dualities" (Bhagavad Gita). All the dualities we face, and therefore all the choices we must make, fit into a dynamic that has less to do with the immediate choice before us and more to do with the future we aspire to.

Chapter 2: The Pursuit of Real Connections

Sometimes we are driven by the needs of others, while at other times we are overwhelmed by the choices we must make independently. We perceive these situations as different only because we have not mastered the art of decision making. For example, selfishness becomes apparent when someone forces us to postpone our own goals in order to fulfill theirs. Once this selfishness is recognized, the person often punishes us for helping. It may sound absurd, but selfish people tend to punish those who help them, as if driven by a force beyond their control. So the decision to help a selfish person is not really a choice. It is less about the help requested and more about the mental state of the person seeking help.

Reflecting on the opportunities we encounter in life, I recall receiving three job offers: one in Europe, another in Asia, and a third after I had already accepted the position in Asia. The European offers were more lucrative financially. However, my decision to go to Asia was not motivated by money, but by the desire to experience different cultures. Therefore, salary and location were irrelevant. During this time, I received numerous job offers from Europe, all with higher salaries, but I always turned them down.

This is often difficult for others to understand because people are generally driven by basic instincts. If they are not motivated by food and sex, they are motivated by money. They make decisions based on these factors and are then surprised by the problems they encounter, often considering people like me lucky. Guided by the pursuit of pleasure and the avoidance of struggle, they fail to understand the deeper meaning of their existence. As a result, they fail to see the opportunities that lie behind the choices they make, often of a less fulfilling nature. Many of the greatest opportunities in my life have come through paths that everyone I met would reject because they required too much work, sacrifice, and risk.

People often lack self-awareness and cannot think beyond their primal instincts, which is why the vast majority are not destined to be wealthy. Their greed, incompetence, lack of insight, lack of motivation to learn, laziness, and lack of honesty drive away anyone who could help them. As such, they live in the paradox of wanting more but not having the qualities that make them deserving. They rarely make decisions based on curiosity, a desire to learn, or love. They focus solely on immediate gratification and survival.

People waste years of their lives that could be better spent preparing for the opportunities they seek, or at least building a network of people they admire, rather than people from whom they seek to extract knowledge and opportunities. The problems they face, which are essentially spiritual in nature, seem normal to them because they have a low level of consciousness. They accept these problems as part of life and summarize their existence with statements that rationalize and justify their choices. They will blame some past event in their life as the cause of their results because they are unable to take responsibility for their own thoughts. They have become so accustomed to this habit that they often have no control over their minds.

When I meet these people, they view me through the same lens because of their mindset. They feign friendship when they want something from me and disappear when they don't find what they're looking for. Many who know me assume that I am wealthy, and when they discover that I don't accumulate the things they value and want, they consider me a failure. These conclusions come from their ignorance because they refuse the opportunity to learn from me. But I mention this not out of arrogance, but from a place of altruism, for I have solutions to the problems they face, but they never want them. Their delusions become part of the arrogance of their character. They refuse to listen, arrogantly believing that they understand me and the reason for our meeting.

Nevertheless, the people we meet and their problems transcend time, making these meetings more than mere coincidences. We attract what is already within us - we receive when we give and we give when we receive. We may not always know what we are offering to others because we are acting from a personal perspective, but our presence and kind words may be exactly what they need.

For example, I travel extensively and spend a lot of time working on books and expect nothing more from others than their company, but they often do not understand this because they do not know the value of freedom. They also don't value kindness, so they completely waste my time with their rudeness. Trying to look smart doesn't impress me, and most people make themselves look foolish, because an intelligent person doesn't feed on brains, but on kindness and honesty. Only the ignorant, the poor, and the uneducated think that social image is more important than character.

Chapter 3: Overcoming Doubt

Many people approach me only when they want something, often ignoring the emotional aspects of friendship. Once they get the information they want, or realize they can't find it, they disappear, unwilling to engage in a mutual exchange. This behavior was particularly surprising when it came to religious people, especially Christians, until I became accustomed to the hypocrisy prevalent among them. Most people are not really looking for religion; they are looking for a group that offers opportunities, higher social status, and the fulfillment of basic needs such as family and procreation. They see religion as a form of community rather than a path to spiritual development, so they readily accept and defend dogma. The dogma becomes part of their identity, just as the community becomes all they have.

But while selfishness is common, selfish individuals are often unhappy because they fail to make real connections. In fact, the more diverse people we meet, the more we realize that unhappiness manifests itself in different forms, all rooted in ignorance, delusion, and selfishness. Only when a person becomes aware of existential dilemmas in an emotional context can it be said that they have evolved from an animal state to a social state. Until then, they are merely human-like primates seeking personal gratification at the expense of others. This does not make them social, but rather psychopaths and narcissists who have found a way to adapt to society.

In our lives, we inevitably encounter people who exploit, use, and humiliate us for their own gratification. These experiences can create obstacles in our personalities that often manifest as doubt. Doubt is like a sweet poison, often administered by those who claim to love us or seek our friendship. When we doubt ourselves, we poison our own personality. Yet the true self - the complete and immortal being - remains within us, dormant, awaiting awakening. This awakening comes through true knowledge, which elevates the mind to a heightened state of awareness. Such knowledge can only be attained by those who are capable of elevating others, and even then one must be willing to receive that elevation.

The immortal soul, though always present, is only revealed as awakened when it encounters a conscious individual. In this state, the individual, previously mired in an animal existence, becomes capable of mastering his instincts by surrendering to the higher self within - the immortal spirit endowed with the ability to see through darkness. This enlightened warrior understands for the first time the purpose of his armor and sword, which have always been there to protect him. They use these tools to slay the dragon of instinct that has long controlled them.

But this dragon never really dies; it reappears with new colors and grotesque faces. This dragon is society itself, corrupted by base instincts. Every being enslaved by instinct and driven by fear - whether it is the instinct to survive and the fear of death, or the need for pleasure and the fear of loneliness - is a diabolical beast, a demon. This is the hell we fear, yet it surrounds us on this planet we call Earth.

The true understanding of our spirit's path - the purpose of our existence, shaped by countless lives leading up to the present moment - is revealed in the reflection of society, with its survival mechanisms and opportunities. This understanding leads to true happiness. But such happiness is never complete, for the physical body suffers, the mind harbors fears, and we remain vulnerable to betrayal, harm, or even murder. However, it is a partial happiness within the diabolic social framework, an anarchic state within a structured system, where we make our own way as social elements. This may involve doing what others consider impossible, living in ways they cannot comprehend, or rejecting habits they consider essential.

When we reach this state of mind, we recognize our value within the system and can easily change it as we acquire new skills and adjust our personalities, all the while understanding the implications for our environment. We are no longer afraid to change our lives, our country, our culture, our lifestyle, or our profession to continue our journey, nor are we afraid to lose our emotional attachments.

The immortality of our soul and accumulated knowledge manifests in these transitions and transformations, especially through interactions with strangers. This is perhaps the quickest way to self-discovery - through communication with others and their reflection of our inner state. For example, we often assume that people don't like us because we don't smile at them, but most people are too ignorant and self-centered to know why they hate someone. They are too absorbed in their own inner world to make correct judgments about others. Their thoughts are nothing more than reflections of their subconscious, which is often filled with unresolved traumas they wish to avoid repeating. Thus, much of the world's hatred is an internal projection of fears and insecurities.

Chapter 4: Transforming Perspectives

The majority of people fear for their survival, which fuels discrimination, racism, and xenophobia. Others fear feeling inferior or unintelligent, which leads them to insult and offend those they perceive as threats or simply smarter than them. I never realized how much animosity people have toward writers until I started answering that I was one when asked about my profession. Most people are unconsciously and deeply ignorant, understanding the world through a practical lens and living in constant fear that their facade will be exposed. They focus on immediate functionality and reject anything that doesn't fit their worldview.

Few transcend this mindset. This is evident in the way they present themselves, often asking about another's job and background in order to form an immediate stereotype to cling to. The entire interaction is then based on these two questions, a common condition of ignorance. It gives the ignorant person the illusion of understanding his interlocutor and forces the stereotype recipient to conform or risk appearing wrong, lost, and ignorant for being different and aware of his uniqueness.

This is why awareness cannot be maintained among ignorant people. The ignorant seek to control others and their environment to reduce their anxiety driven by insecurities, so they never risk going beyond what they know. Their conversations are driven by an obsession to control communication through preconceived notions of what to ask and answer in order to appear normal. Through their fear-based thinking and communication, they keep themselves right where they are, no matter how much they claim to desire change. Decades and even a lifetime will pass and you will see them right where they have always been, thinking the same, doing the same, assuming the same. In fact, they will talk to you according to the image they have of you, assuming that just as they never change, you never have.

Have you ever had the experience of talking to someone who doesn't really see you? If your family members don't feel uncomfortable with you, and especially if they love you as you are, you must be doing something wrong with your life, because it means you haven't changed enough to confuse them.

We cannot always make the right decisions, especially under time pressure. However, the more we integrate knowledge and truth into our personalities, the more natural and correct our decisions become, even in the most difficult times. A martial artist understands this concept well. They learn to react in different situations that rarely occur in everyday life, but this awareness of danger enables them to avoid conflicts and make better decisions in other contexts. The greatest benefit of practicing martial arts is the control of fear, which is the emotion that most often prevents us from acting correctly in life and exploring new environments.

Learning about life provides numerous opportunities to understand new perspectives at any time. If we consider that our mind works by adapting to the patterns of reality that it can represent, we can verify that the awareness of truth is limited by only three factors:

- Lack of knowledge about the elements that influence our lives;

- Misunderstanding the interactions between the different elements of our reality;

- Incorrect assimilation of the elements of reality that interfere with the structure that makes it up on a universal and timeless level.

Learning has a similar effect in each of these cases, as it represents the recognition of new contexts of reality that influence how we observe, shape, and then restructure our identity. Our sense of self is intimately connected to our perception and understanding of reality. How we see others defines who we are as a person and how we think about our role in society. This understanding gradually eliminates the feeling of unresolved problems, although they do not cease to exist. It is an operation that leads to the discharge of negative energies through the purification and renewal of those that already exist through consciousness. In other words, it's not so much what happened to you in the past, but your understanding of it and how it has affected your current life path.

The past cannot be changed, but the way we assimilate that past to strengthen the possibility of a better future can. If you've been unfairly attacked, insulted, lost something important in your life, or made mistakes that have taken your life in a new direction, what matters now is how far you can continue to exist with the same personality you had before such events. What really matters are your dreams, and you can always dream new dreams. For those who have faith, nothing else is needed. However, those who have everything and yet have no faith cannot be helped when the time comes to make difficult decisions, because their emotional possessions and attachments are all they have, and these cannot remain in the face of the transformations that fate imposes.

Chapter 5: The Masks of Social Conformity

During World War II, many people refused to believe the stories of Nazi atrocities and were reluctant to leave their homes and livelihoods. But a visit to a concentration camp in Poland - a country that still struggles with racism - reveals the stark reality of that era. This disconnect between past and present persists, as people often recount historical events as if they were distant memories, failing to recognize their continuing relevance.

I once visited a country where the behavior of the citizens was so aberrant that it seemed almost alien. Their actions were so psychotic that the entire nation resembled a mental institution, with everyone experiencing the same delusions and perceiving their behavior as normal. Fascinatingly, visitors from other countries often assimilated these habits and excused them as cultural norms. In their eagerness to integrate, foreigners accepted these traits as typical, inadvertently normalizing behaviors that should have been criticized and rejected.

When I began to question these observable behaviors, I was accused of being negative, unfriendly, and incapable of integrating into the culture. The majority saw me as the problem. But who was really at fault in this scenario-me or the culture?

If I had blindly followed the crowd, I might have assumed they were right and I was wrong. Instead, I delved into the history of the region. I discovered that when the Teutonic Knights invaded the area in 1411, they found people still practicing human sacrifice. Yes, as late as 1411, these people were burning their own alive and hanging them to honor pagan gods. Furthermore, when the Nazis invaded in 1945, they didn't need concentration camps because the citizens were betraying their own neighbors - people they had considered friends for years. I also learned that this highly xenophobic and racist country has one of the highest suicide rates in the world. So, in a culture steeped in human sacrifice, suicide, and prejudice, I was told that I was the one who was wrong. Remember that the next time a large group tells you you're wrong about something - sometimes even millions of people can miss the obvious. This example, concerning the territory of Lithuania in Europe, is just one of many around the world.

Numerous psychological studies have shown that most people tend to change their behavior and thinking, even resorting to dishonesty, in order to conform to the actions of others. As a result, you often find yourself surrounded by people who spout nonsense. The more you associate with such people, the more absurdity you'll encounter. The only viable solution is to allow those who believe they're right (and you're wrong) to continue to exist in their comfortable, delusional world while you move on with your life. You won't be able to change the billions who act this way, nor the people you know who follow the crowd and base their opinions on the majority.

Many avoid critical thinking because it involves responsibility and the freedom to own one's thoughts, which can be intimidating. As a result, it's easier for them to rationalize any fact based on the belief that the majority is always right. In essence, the majority doesn't think independently, but rationalizes observations based on group morality. This is the source of their concepts of right and wrong. Often you're not dealing with a truly conscious human being, but with a living being that lacks an awakened soul - a kind of "undead". I've observed similar behavior in various cultures and religions, which has helped me to understand the limitations of people's perspectives.

You cannot change the ignorant, but you can learn from them. For example, you can see that most people are beyond hope; they will cling to their thoughts all their lives because they are resistant to change. Spending time with them is not only futile, but also harmful to your self-confidence. In addition, many people I know, including family members, would become angry with me because they believed that the world they knew from television was more real than my firsthand experience. They were convinced that they were right because they had seen, for example, an hour-long television program about Finland, and they believed that I, who had actually been to Finland and had a different opinion, was wrong.

I had the same problem with my opinions about China, which they only knew from television. They thought that I, who lived in China at the time, was either lying about everything or didn't know China as well as they did because they had learned everything from television. It's amazing and almost unbelievable how ignorant people can be. But then you realize that you're not surrounded by individuals capable of meaningful conversation, but by people who mindlessly follow the crowd.

The vast majority of people are in a truly deplorable state of mind. However, the world of the ignorant is not the world of the successful. You must learn to deal with the disappointment, betrayal, lies, manipulation, and abandonment of those who truly believe they are right and consider themselves great and positive individuals.

Chapter 6: The Herd Mentality

The minds of the truly ignorant are often filled with delusional ideas about themselves. To them, anyone who challenges their beliefs is considered insane. They are determined to prevent others from succeeding in ways different from their own, because such success would highlight their failures. They see the world as a competition in which the concept of being or doing anything different is almost non-existent. Their thoughts are shaped by what they perceive the majority to be right or wrong.

If you achieve what others think is impossible, they will rationalize reasons to discredit your accomplishments. They may argue that you cheated, stole your knowledge, or just got lucky and don't deserve your success. They will never acknowledge the hours you worked or the books you read because these facts do not fit their world view.

These people often believe that all wealthy people either stole, cheated, or just got lucky. This is the mental world in which they live. Many people I meet around the world assume I'm stealing information for my books or profiting from something illegal, while others think I'm just lucky to be able to write and make a living at it. They believe that my knowledge is easily accessible and that I can get rich just by sharing my thoughts. They lack an understanding of what is real versus fantasy, practical knowledge versus worthless opinion, and the distinction between what requires study and what can be expressed as mere personal opinion. They are unaware of the intellectual effort involved in effective thinking and information analysis. They lack the tools and are unaware of their existence. They truly believe that someone like me can write nonsense and sell it to readers. That is the world they live in.

For many, this world is so real that they refuse to believe what I write, even if they buy my books. It's disheartening to witness such ignorance, but that's the reality of living in a world where people are blind and remain in the dark all their lives. I've met many people who have spent their lives searching for answers but refuse to read the solutions I offer in my books. They think they are smarter than me and continue to look for answers in all the wrong places.

Interestingly, they judge knowledge and intelligence by appearances and only validate the information that fits their stereotypes. This wouldn't be such a blatant display of their ignorance if they weren't mistaken about their chosen mentors and their ability to understand them. As many ancient religious texts suggest, God keeps the arrogant blind so that they will never see the secrets they don't deserve.

The arrogant are completely blinded by the superficial world presented to them. This worldview is reinforced daily by their observations and habits. They cannot change; they have been metaphorically turned to stone, as if hypnotized by the Medusa of the illusory world. They are mentally stagnant, and their rationalizations are mere byproducts of their state of mind, as if they are only imagining that they are thinking. Over time, their unwillingness to think becomes a handicap as they lose the ability to discriminate and see beyond their beliefs. They become trapped in their own worldview, forever doomed to failure. Their failure becomes the norm.

The vast majority of people believe they are thinking, but they are not. When confronted with their ignorance, they are often offended. This is because they are so deeply convinced of the lies they live by that they cannot bear to be told they are completely wrong. The most effective prison is the belief that one is free, when in fact one is a prisoner of one's own fears and thoughts. Since most people do not really think, but only rationalize what the herd thinks is right, their fears mirror those of the herd. They fear a wolf they have never seen and trust the shepherds who exploit them - their leaders, politicians, priests and others.

We can observe clear differences in people through their communication styles. A person may perceive themselves as antisocial or struggle with communication because of the behavior of others toward them and the accusations they face as a result of accumulated frustrations in their interactions. Whenever someone thinks differently than the majority, the majority, with its herd mentality, assumes that the minority is wrong and tries in various ways to bring them back into the fold.

Chapter 7: The Dynamics of Conformity

When people try to change my way of thinking and fail, they often feel uncomfortable and insulted. They feel they are making a positive effort while labeling me as antisocial. Rarely do they consider that they may be violating my identity or dismissing my analyses. Essentially, because I analyze things differently, I am considered wrong because I do not agree with the majority. Their agreement with the majority and their rationalization of their opinions leads them to value these justifications over my analysis.

This scenario mirrors several studies on the psychology of peer pressure, where individuals have been shown to change their opinions to conform to the group's view, even when they know they are wrong. For example, if a group insists that something real is not true, an individual, despite disagreeing, feels compelled to conform to the group. If a new member disagrees, the individual from the previous situation will persuade the newcomer to adopt the group's behavior-behavior that he initially knew to be wrong but now accepts as right.

Numerous experiments have shown how easily people can be manipulated. Interestingly, those who think they are smarter than others are often the easiest to manipulate, precisely because they feel the most pressure to be a "good boy". They seek the approval of others, so they conform to what seems right in order to achieve that goal. When tyrannical governments and organizations realized how easily they could change the behavior of the majority by associating the "good boy" idea with the desired behavior, revolutions were easily ignited and ideologies such as communism emerged. Today, in countries like China, we are witnessing the power of this factor. The Chinese government has established a point system for the population, where the "good citizen" is the one who accumulates many points, instilling fear of being "different" and increasing the oppression they already endure.

It is remarkably easy to control a population that is afraid to think differently. Influenced by the media and their desire for social acceptance, people tend to judge reality by appearances and accept that reality as truth. When faced with a multitude of choices, they prioritize trends and form a view of reality that aligns with the majority - the so-called social mass. Consequently, anything different is met with prejudice. People judge what is different negatively in order to reduce their anxiety and exclude the behavior or person exhibiting it.

Before analysis, what is different triggers an automatic and instinctive response. Thus, the mental prison created by beliefs is later reinforced by the fear of difference. The more fear a person accumulates, the more their ability to think diminishes to the point where they are virtually incapable of rationalizing even the most elementary tasks. Their world shrinks to a routine of habits-eating, working, sleeping, and walking in the garden near home on weekends. It's a life not unlike that of their pets, which perhaps explains why they see so much of themselves in their animals.

Consider a person who takes a course in communication and learns all the elements of effective communication. With this knowledge, they draw conclusions through comparative analysis and deduction. They come to understand that those they accuse of ignorance share the same contextual characteristics-assumptions that are not necessarily concrete truths, but rather perceived truths. This realization transforms individuals as they begin to understand who they are, or who they aspire to be, within their social context. They realize that much of what others perceive is filtered through systems of prejudice.

People analyze the present based on their past and are slow to adopt new ways of thinking because they fear being different. At this level of interpretation, communication cannot take place without a conflict of interest. This is why people who read widely often have difficulty communicating with those who are ignorant. Ignorant people tend to rationalize based on what they believe to be true. Yet often the most ignorant people seem to be successful in business. They live in a truth that works for them, yet they feel miserable inside. In the end, it all comes down to a person's values.

Chapter 8: The Complexity of Moral Standards

A person with high moral standards often finds it difficult to adapt to a lifestyle that prioritizes financial gain over personal happiness. This development is often accompanied by ridicule, ostracism, and discrimination. Much of the guilt we experience is tied to fear - fear of rejection, fear of loss, and fear of opposition from family or friends. Guilt is such a powerful, fear-inducing emotion that many people use it to prevent us from changing, with phrases like "Think of your children" or "How can you let your parents down?" Many also internalize this guilt, engaging in inner dialogues such as "I must think of my children" or "I can't let my parents down".

Guilt can become an impenetrable barrier to the pursuit of success. Many people do not consider alternatives until they have exhausted all options, such as leaving their children with family members for a year or two to provide better conditions and support the parents with a higher income, not just a physical presence. Most people do not think long term and waste many years of their lives. However, the most significant changes always take time and involve high risks that cannot be overcome if we cling to too many emotional attachments.

Think of your emotional attachments as objects on a boat. When strong waves hit, if your boat cannot float easily, these objects can cause it to sink. The same is true in our lives, although we do not want to equate the people we love with objects. For example, for much of my life I had to leave friends behind in order to achieve my goals. I always hoped that these friends would not forget me, but they often did. This experience taught me that no one is really anyone's friend. The vast majority of people are only friends with themselves. What you bring to them through friendship is only valid with your presence. This is not always the case, but in most situations it is.

In almost every situation where people I have not seen in many years have wanted to talk to me, it has been because they wanted something - a job, a business opportunity, something they needed - rather than because they felt a real connection. That connection has happened with maybe ten people out of more than 10,000 I have met in 15 years. It is very easy for me to make new friends. People are always amazed at how quickly I make new friends in any country. But in the end, out of these many friendships, there may be one or none with whom I continue to communicate. Most people do not empathize with anyone. Their concept of friendship is based on ego: "What can others do for me?"

We can observe this in a group of people. The best-dressed man and the most beautiful woman are always surrounded by people who want sex and money. Unfortunately, with very few exceptions, these are all the people in the group. However, the individuals that no one wants to talk to are often the most interesting, and most people cannot see this. Whenever I communicate with someone others despise, they assume I want something from that person. If it is a woman, they think it is sex. If it is a man, they think it is work-related.

Most people have a very limited view of the world because of their ego. The more self-centered they are, the narrower their view of the world. This is because of the need to survive. The more people believe their survival is threatened, the more they behave that way. In other words, small-minded, short-sighted people are more self-centered.

We could call this materialism, but even materialism is nothing more than an obsession with survival. The person who has nothing always thinks he is poor. That is why many people are confused when they realize that I do not have much. My life is very simple because I am always getting rid of clothes and things to maintain that simplicity. This frightens people because it creates a dissociation in their brain between two elements that they thought were connected.

Many people misunderstand the true purpose of wealth. It's not to indulge in more food, to buy more cars and watches, or to display photos of trips to exotic places. The most valuable purpose of wealth is freedom. Freedom is intangible; it is the power to do what you want, when you want. This concept is so foreign to most people that they often don't understand when I answer their question: "How long do you plan to stay in this city?" Not one of the dozens of people I've met in every city I've visited has understood the answer "because I want to." They always react as if I'm lying and withholding the truth. They cannot understand that there is a person who can enter and leave a country at will, without any plan. This idea is completely foreign to their worldview because it implies a level of freedom they have never seen, heard of, or even thought possible.

Many people I meet around the world are unfamiliar with the concept of making money in their sleep. They assume that all money is earned through work, that it takes time to accumulate wealth, and that it must be acquired by staying in one place. If someone doesn't follow this path, they suspect criminal activity. Some people are so skeptical that they think I'm a criminal. They refuse to believe that I'm just more knowledgeable because of an education they didn't choose. So I often say that ignorance is a choice. I feel justified in calling the people I refer to in my books idiots, imbeciles, and stupid, because what took me over 20 years to understand, through hundreds of books and studies, as well as personal experience, is summarized in my writings, and yet these individuals refuse to read them, thinking they are already wise. This arrogance, coupled with ignorance, is the epitome of stupidity. When I tell someone that I've documented everything I know and they choose not to read it, they are too blind to see the obvious.

Chapter 9: The Fear of Change

The solution to the ignorance of the majority, even the poorest, is often just a book away. I understand that finding the right book can be a challenge, but we've all had to read many wrong books to discover the right ones. People who only read bestsellers and books recommended by friends still don't understand this, because they try to avoid mistakes by consuming popularized nonsense. The most popular books often contain the most common sense.

You will rarely find a truly insightful book on the bestseller shelves because such books are not accepted by the majority. Most people look for books that bolster their ego, not those that challenge, attack, or dismantle it. So when someone tells me that they read a lot, but only famous authors, I know that person will never progress in life. They are afraid of making mistakes and confronting their ego. This is the fate of such people. They read a lot, but it's as if they don't know anything. I see it in their conversations. They have knowledge, but they lack practical skills.

This problem is widespread in universities, where vast subjects are taught without practical application. Universities follow the same principles of intellectualizing knowledge. I know this because I was a university professor, and I quickly understood how the system works. Many university professors are burdened with outdated and useless knowledge, but they think they're smarter than others because they've never done anything that doesn't conform to social norms. They mistake the attention they get from students - hypocritical, exam-based, fear-driven attention - for real value.

But I always took a different approach, which often intimidated my students, who asked, "What's on the exam?" "Why are you discussing so many different topics?" I would tell them: "Everything I say is vital to your existence". The test is just a moment in that existence. If you understand me correctly, there's no need to study for the test, because you will realize how everything I say applies to real life. My goal is for you to be successful in life, not just in exams.

Very few students understood this. Most remained fixated on the test. As mentioned earlier, many people have a limited view of reality and miss many opportunities. Students who saw me only as a teacher and couldn't see the person behind the profession were wasting their time. They didn't waste my time because I was compensated, but much of what I shared that was ignored is in my books. They don't read them because they are no longer my students, and that is another form of ignorance-wasting the opportunity to learn from the same person over a lifetime.

There are people who grasp the truth in five minutes, others who take five years, and some who take fifty years. However, consciousness evolves only through the choices that create change, not the time it takes to change: the books we read, the decisions we make, the journeys we take, the people we meet, the risks we take, and the changes we implement. Without these actions, nothing else matters-not even the problems we think are important-because everything can change with a single choice. Behind the most valuable choices lie the real issues: fear of losing people-friends, family, etc.; fear of change; fear of failure; lack of self-esteem; fear of being alone; fear of trusting the wrong people; fear of betrayal.

In addition, most fears are tied to past experiences and don't always have a reason to persist. One such fear is the fear of starting over. This fear is different for a 20-year-old who knows little about life than it is for a 50-year-old who has lived longer and is more adept at adapting to new situations and environments. But many people never find answers to their dilemmas, even in life, because of their inability to adapt. Yet discovering the necessary answers can lead to radical and transformative changes in their lives, the very changes that frighten them.

The reason many people don't find the answers they are looking for is because they are afraid to find them. For example, many people I've met have asked me to teach them how to create and run an online business, only to later offer trivial excuses for giving up, such as "I don't know how to pay taxes," "I need to register the business first," or "I'll try to get financial help from the government". The excuses for giving up are numerous, far more than the ones I've mentioned, because, as I've observed, people are incredibly creative in the art of failure. They know many ways to fail, but almost none to succeed.

Chapter 10: The Success Triangle

The most common way people set themselves up for failure is through laziness. For example, I once asked someone to work with me on children's books. It took her over three months to create a single story. The project dragged on until she lost her job, and then she used the job search as an excuse to stop working on what I had asked her to do. Three months would have been enough time to finish at least one book. Instead, she did nothing-absolutely nothing-except waste time. Unfortunately, these scenarios are all too common. People make up stories to waste time and distract themselves from their goals. Then, when months go by and nothing is accomplished, they claim they can't continue because there are no profits and some external event has diverted their attention.

Of course, there are no profits when there is no productivity, and you assume you will live for a thousand years, oblivious to the world moving faster than you. They should realize this if they choose to be lazy, but laziness reinforces the idea of stagnation, which is why people find it so relaxing. In fact, it seems that people are as attracted to failure as they are to pleasure and stagnation.

Psychology talks about the conscious and the subconscious, but the distinction isn't as clear-cut as it seems. Many people fail from the moment they make a conscious decision because they never believed they could succeed. These same people later claim that people like me were just lucky, because it's easier to say that than to take responsibility.

Of course, if you don't work or do anything for months, you need a lot of luck to get results. It's also true that such luck is more likely with 30 children's stories than with just one. People who say I'm very lucky overlook the fact that I've published more than 200 books in five languages, produced more than 600 songs, and founded more than 10 companies in my lifetime. That's over a thousand books and various companies with various products in less than 20 years. I have also been a consultant for several companies and worked in several universities, often at the same time. I am not lucky - far from it - considering the huge amount of work produced.

There is much more work than luck in the whole cycle of success, but those who believe in luck don't believe in work. That's why they say, "You're very lucky!" You must think that I wrote a book based on a personal opinion and repeated it hundreds of times with different words. Stupidity is related to laziness, but even a hard-working person will eventually stop being stupid. If you're really ignorant, but you read 100 pages of any book every day, you won't remain ignorant. The power of consciousness transcends the limitations of materiality; it can transform both it and us on the same plane and simultaneously.

It is in the triangulation between matter, self-realization and consciousness that every dream manifests and every transformation becomes possible. The emotions felt when this happens are accompanied by a vision of true freedom. The freedom that every being seeks is manifested as we overcome the challenges of life. The more we work in this direction, the more we feel this sense of accomplishment. We might even say that the faster we work toward our goals, the more likely we are to achieve them. This persistence and speed comes at the cost of time, but here we find another triangle of manifestation, this time related to action. Effective action that leads to success is thus translated into a triangle of persistence, speed, and sacrifice.

Persistence and speed are concepts that are easy to understand. Sacrifice, however, is often misunderstood, so it is crucial to explain its connection to pleasure. When maximum pleasure is derived from the use of substances such as alcohol, sugar, tobacco, and unhealthy foods, sacrifice becomes obvious. The next level involves the sacrifice of time, especially time spent on pleasurable activities such as watching television, playing games, and socializing. Then comes the sacrifice associated with persevering beyond self-doubt and lower emotions. As we go deeper, we encounter the physical level of suffering, where the signs of physical, psychological, and emotional pain appear. Here we confront our inner demons, the memories of the past, and especially the traumas we had hoped to forget. But the ultimate sacrifice is one that is felt in one's own body as one struggles against the limitations imposed by pain, hunger, exhaustion, and sleep deprivation.

This is not to say that the sacrifices we endure cannot be compensated for in a way that avoids the pain. But here the sacrifice is explained as the need for more discipline, because discipline is what keeps you focused on your goals. A driver who isn't focused can't race, an Olympic athlete who isn't focused won't win a gold medal, and a soldier who isn't focused can lose his life. The focus of these individuals comes from years of dedication and consistent discipline.

Chapter 11: Discipline and Spiritual Development

When discussing perseverance and motivation, we often overlook the fact that they cannot exist without discipline-both mental and physical. If we are going to spend countless hours in front of a computer or reading in order to achieve our goals, we must maintain the same level of discipline through physical activity. Whether it's a group sport or exercises we can do in moderation at home, the more discipline we build into our lives, the more naturally our brains will focus on tasks. Jumping rope at home is perhaps the easiest and most effective exercise. I aim to jump at least 100 to 200 times a day, as fast as I can, because it helps with coordination, endurance, discipline, and both physical and heart health.

We can overcome existential barriers through spiritual progress and physical activity. In other words, we do not overcome difficulties by merely observing them or exchanging opinions with others, but by contemplating the future and working diligently toward the goals we envision. Experience always changes the subject's relationship to reality and, by extension, to himself. The way we feel and interpret the world is significantly changed by experience. Thus, the knowledge gained through learning and discipline allows for a higher level of consciousness-more wisdom and, consequently, spiritual evolution. This spiritual evolution is not only internal; you will see manifestations of it in the world around you. In fact, as you expand your mind, your ability to see opportunities that can change your future will become more apparent. We can only see what we are ready to see.

Spiritual evolution occurs whenever the mind develops its awareness through interaction with the physical world, but this interaction is expanded through determination, persistence, discipline, and knowledge. However, because human beings typically form their personalities based on how they are judged by their reality, they often fail to see possibilities for themselves beyond what the world presents. Our independence in choosing values and making decisions is strongly influenced by the opinions of our family, culture, and social circles. It is also revealed in the contrast of opposites, which means that we are presented daily with choices that can change the events of the following days.

Once you realize the illusion presented within this duality, you will be able to transcend your challenges. You will see that there is nothing wrong with opposing others or making them believe that you are wrong. You will stop blaming yourself for others' inability to understand you, which often manifests as self-punishment in the form of resentment. In fact, it is desirable and expected that when we reach a higher level of morality, the majority of the population will despise, insult, and oppose us because we represent a contrast to their worldview and a threat to the worldviews they cling to.

Although most thoughts are essentially derived from choices associated with group conformity, usually imposed subliminally - and becoming explicit when they cannot be controlled subliminally - conscious behaviors are those which the individual recognizes as his own, even if copied from his group. This differentiation occurs when the individual can oppose and transcend his own thoughts with decisions that go against his intuition, beliefs, and habits because he perceives a better outcome awaiting him.

From this perspective, we cannot analyze problems as effectively as we can see them in relational logic, because most of our problems are more about personal perception than reality itself. Many personal problems can be automatically eliminated with a change of perspective or expansion of consciousness. This is evident when we move from one country to another and encounter a different culture dealing with similar issues. The world is so interconnected, and most people are so averse to change, that you can learn a great deal about yourself simply by changing your environment.

Often you will also find that many opinions formed and accepted about the world and our personalities are typically the result of the views of one or two people, usually those with whom we spend the most time, not to mention the media, where television is prominent. The opinion of one person can be captured by millions as the holder of unquestionable truth. Most people are still easily swayed by what the media tells them to believe. But as we rise above the thoughts and opinions of the masses through the formation of self-identity and self-awareness, our karmic cycles become smaller and shorter.   44

Chapter 12: The Dynamics of Karma

In today's fast-paced world, our lives change rapidly and our problems seem to solve themselves more quickly. We possess a power that many find incomprehensible-the ability to completely alter our destiny in a matter of months with nothing more than thoughts, information, and incremental decisions adjusted for unpredictable outcomes. However, until we accept that our minds hold the solutions to all our problems, we may face numerous disappointments and lose friendships. This is often because our challenges, the people we meet, and our various fears stem from karmic issues that we need to resolve. We continue to attract the people and experiences necessary for self-reflection, even when we encounter the worst people in society. These encounters force us to confront our lack of self-love and our need for self-validation through the pursuit of life goals that many have deemed unattainable or beyond our abilities.

The outer world is always a reflection of the inner world, though not always in a direct or opposite way. We may experience disappointment only to realize that we should be more proactive in seeking out valuable friendships - quicker to sever low-value connections and more eager to pursue new ones. The more active we are in this process of seeking respect and love, the more quickly we attract it. Conversely, when we need such lessons, we attract what we need to learn and continue to suffer until the lessons are understood.

When people face problems but deny responsibility, they often look to others for solutions, as if others know better what their lives need. The truth is that most people are full of opinions, usually based on rationalizations of their own experiences, but they understand little about how life really works. As a result, the vast majority oscillate between contentment and despair. Despair comes when life changes and they don't know how to adapt. Many people spend years focusing their energies on controlling their social appearances rather than evolving and becoming better individuals. They understand very little about the world, and as a result, manifestations of spiritual suffering are not genuine requests for help.

We see this when we help someone who asks for help, only to be insulted by them later. This is more likely the more we try to help, because most of the problems people create in their lives are intentional. It's like the games they choose to play. For example, a person who says, "I can't travel because I have a job," may not want to start their own business for fear of failure, using the job as an excuse to deny themselves something they want. People often choose one element of their reality to justify their choices. It's a way of shifting the blame from within to an external factor, something that cannot be connected to their own choices. So every time we offer a solution to someone who has created a problem in their life, we are denying them the karma they have created through their own beliefs.

Karma is created by the individual to have a game to play in what they call life, and when we take that game away from people, they resent us because we have taken the meaning out of their spiritual existence, no matter how dramatic and painful it may seem. They need the problems they have created in order to understand themselves. We can't help them by removing the problems, because they will quickly seek new ones. Instead, we must give them more similar problems to help them accelerate this progress. This may sound cruel until you realize that the most effective mind therapy is to get the individual to confront and talk about their own fears, even to find creative ways to process more reasons for the fears, which will eventually lead them to understand why they created them.

It is only when the individual realizes that he has controlled and created his entire life, and understands why, that he is truly liberated. Ironically, the more ignorant a person is, the more problems he needs in life to feel that his life is important. The humble person rarely feels the need to have problems because they have invalidated their sense of importance by accumulating wisdom. They are invisible to those who seek problems and ways to feel important in society. We call this karma only because the individual is responsible for the same problems he attracts. Karma is not something outside the individual's character or beliefs. It is quite ironic that the less fear you have, the less others want to confront you. So we can assume that a person who attracts confrontation believes that he must be afraid for some strange reason. Some may even say that fear and anxiety fuel their motivation to become better individuals, as if their illness is complementary to their spiritual ascension.

Chapter 13: The Illusion of Change and the Comfort of Problems

When we remove problems from people's lives, it can feel as if we are preventing them from achieving their goals. For this reason, many people prefer to be medicated with psychotropic drugs to help them cope with their challenges rather than make complete lifestyle changes. If you are very effective at eliminating someone's problems, they may feel that they are losing their autonomy and individualism, however illusory that may be. They may react with statements like, "You think you know everything, but you don't know me," or "That's just your opinion". They may even try to dissuade you by saying, "My case is different from everyone else's," and accuse you of manipulation with statements like, "You can't know what to do because you haven't been in my shoes".

A woman once asked me if I was manipulating her, and when I asked why, she replied, "Because I always feel very comfortable around you". Obviously, she was attached to the need to feel disrespected, humiliated, and abandoned, which is why our relationship didn't last. She was looking for drama, not the stability she claimed to want. Many people claim to want something while resisting it because they are not being honest with themselves. As a result, what they say and do often reflects their inner issues more than your actions or words.

Most people aren't ready to change and may never be, which is why they have problems that seem to last forever. Instead, they form an identity around these problems and reorganize their lives so that the problems continue to exist. That's why when people can't get the partners they want, they have to accept the ones they get. If they can't travel to places they can't afford, they tell themselves it's because they're poor, not because they need to rethink their life choices. It's interesting how people rationalize their poverty, often associating it with their country, because they can't admit that they don't want to change their circumstances to get different results. They may even use family as an excuse to never change, as if it were better to be poor in company than rich alone.

The only answer such people can accept is one that doesn't exist, because it is an answer that doesn't require any change in themselves or their reality. They want to stay the way they are forever, and they often do, even after they die. A ghost is nothing more than a stubborn soul that refuses to leave the planet or reincarnate, preferring instead to repeat the same habits it had in life for many more centuries, including traumas that no longer make sense after so much time has passed. True horror, as a more extreme form of evil, always comes from an addiction to trauma.

Anyone who loves self-pity and self-validation through traumas that no longer prevent him from improving his life is halfway there and heading for that hell.

When such people ask me how I make money, they don't want to know how many hours I spend writing or how many books I've read. They just want a magic answer that will allow them to pull knowledge out of thin air and create a book instantly without any effort. But they also insult you in the same way. When I decided to quit my job as a manager and consultant for important companies and become a security guard, my friends were confused and my own mother said, "Finally you have a job that suits you. I hope you can stay there forever."

I spent every day and night during my shifts reading, and I never read so much in my life. I also wrote my first books on the job. About a year later, I changed jobs again. This time I worked as a professor in China and traveled to various countries in Asia. At that time I received even more criticism from my family and realized that the best solution was not a choice, but karma that I had to accept: I had to stop talking to them all. Since I stopped responding to their messages, I have made much more money than ever before. Karma truly affects us in more ways than we can imagine, but most importantly in how our energy attracts the dreams that seem out of reach, especially when we dedicate years and tremendous hours of hard work to get there.

The more people are immersed in their karmic cycles, the less able they are to accept conflicting answers from others, and the more they are involved in making sure they are accepted by people who may not have their best interests at heart. Therefore, it is said that understanding a problem is not as important as understanding yourself. Many problems can be easily eliminated by asking yourself these questions:

- "What would happen if my life didn't have this problem? Would it be worse?"

- "What would happen if my life had no problems? Would it be boring?"

The reason these questions are so powerful comes from the conflicting ideas people have about controlling their destiny. Many people tell me that predicting the future makes life boring, and they don't want to know what's going to happen all the time. They want to insist on rejecting the connection between personal responsibility and the consequences of that responsibility. They refuse to take control of their karmic cycles. And they don't seem to care how their actions and words affect their future. That's what they're really rejecting when they say they don't want to know the future.

Whenever people try to know the future by guessing, they are always trying to predict something inevitable, as if they could take shortcuts in life and escape the problems they create. They never want to know how they are creating that future. Whenever someone has asked me to see their future, they have never wanted me to tell them how to create that future. They want to know the effect, not the cause, so they keep repeating the same karmic cycles. And then they say that futurology doesn't work because their lives never change. Of course, life doesn't change if a person refuses to

look in the mirror of the soul and accept the mistakes he has made
as his own.

Chapter 14: The Lonely Journey of the Soul

We are born and die alone. The friends we make in life are other souls we cross paths with, and when we are reborn we may meet some of them again, although the chances are slim. Most spiritual beings embark on a solitary journey of individual development in the world. This journey validates their personal worth and transforms them through their experiences. They lose more of their attachments and the people they love if they are brave enough to change quickly. However, we gradually transform ourselves through experiences of polarities and dualities, through pain and pleasure, as we interact in a reality that later influences our identity.

We must develop an equal capacity to withstand pain and let go of pleasure if we are to gain more from life. This capacity is balanced by the competence we have accumulated, which remains with us in the transition between lives. We always become better versions of ourselves simply by moving beyond the dualities and our thoughts of what they represent to us. It is the ability to be wrong and the humility to accept the unknowns that help us cross the boundaries between the possible and the impossible and reach for possibilities we could never imagine. It comes with love for ourselves and our purpose as spiritual beings. It means finding a life so full of meaning that we accept the process of suffering as much as we love the joy that accompanies it, not as stagnant states of being, but as experiences that push us to become better people and more fulfilled.

We must work to create the same kind of life on earth that we expect to find after death. To integrate the concept of paradise as a place where we are reborn to enjoy a more peaceful life, we must also consider reincarnation. This is how we embrace the meaning of our existence and purpose as a soul beyond the circumstances that force us to adopt a particular culture and physical appearance. Reincarnation becomes more meaningful when we no longer have reasons to be reborn on earth, when we are proud of what we have left behind and understand what it means to be a planetary being, not attached to any territory. It doesn't mean that we won't have problems on Earth if we want to return, because there will always be various challenges. But it does mean that we understand why they exist and why others create them.

Understanding the causes of ignorance frees us from the mistakes of others and the negative emotions they create in us. This knowledge elevates our mind within a single lifetime. As we learn to perceive reality from different perspectives, we also realize our role in it and learn to detach. This process may require moments of solitude, which are significant for what they represent: an opportunity to begin anew and to understand ourselves better. When your desire to socialize comes not from a fear of being alone, but from a genuine interest in meeting interesting and compassionate people with whom to share kindness, you understand this truth from a more holistic and authentic perspective. You also learn to listen to others for what they believe, not just what they say.

Most people lack awareness of their words, even though everything they say has its own context. People are guided by emotions, like fish in the ocean, following their immediate instincts based on their experiences. But the awareness that transcends time and physical appearances and exists between souls is what spiritual elevation truly reveals. It's when you understand the meaning of "God is everywhere" and recognize yourself in this divine vision. Through this awareness, the greatest truths sporadically and consistently manifest in our minds. The hidden becomes increasingly visible, allowing us to perceive the laws of existence that are common to all living beings.

Although it is challenging for empathetic individuals to witness the suffering of others, and you become more empathetic as you grow in higher awareness, this suffering is part of a global order that is essential to the context that supports it. It is created for individuals to reach new levels of consciousness. Humans literally attract and create their own problems, which becomes clear when one analyzes their history and examines the choices that have led them to their current state. This is especially interesting when we look at the historical and global patterns that have set the stage for the fall of many tribes and nations.

For many who cannot see the light, only an abundance of darkness can create the need for enlightenment to allow them to accept what lies beyond themselves. In this abundance of darkness, the ego is suppressed and the soul is revealed. However, the result is not always positive and can often be traumatic. Many people commit suicide on their way to Ascension. This is why meditation is crucial, or at least moments of solitude to reflect on our past, experiences and choices. The more you do this, the more you understand the context in which you find yourself and the reasons for the conflicts and challenges in your life. It is not always necessary that you learn to accept what happens to you; it is often more important that you learn to love yourself.

Chapter 15: Life in Three-Year Increments

To gain insight during moments of inner contemplation, consider dividing your life into three-year increments and reflecting on the following questions What were your greatest challenges during those three years? Who did you encounter who tried to prevent you from achieving certain goals and who helped you? How did these interactions go? What were the most important lessons you learned?

In my personal experience over the past three years, I've learned that the people who hurt me the most were the people I loved the most. My biggest challenges have been financial, stemming from mistakes in past decisions. The people who helped me the most were not individuals, but my beliefs and knowledge that changed everything. As a result, I became more independent and realized that I needed to be more decisive in my decisions and spend less time with people who were blind to the value I offered. I hadn't realized these lessons for the previous three years. I had too many unproductive friendships and wasted time with these people when I could have gained more from my own determination.

From one three-year period to the next, the karma that accumulated was clearly related to a lack of determination and the need to be quicker in selecting and rejecting the people I allow into my life. Today I am much less patient with people because I can clearly see when they are wasting my time. The next step will be a continuation of this learning that will include choosing the best city to live in and put down roots for a while. This step is about healing the heart. So far my experiences have been mostly spiritual, so it doesn't matter how others judge us when they say we think too much or should feel more, because each of us is at our own stage of development. But as we gather enough knowledge to achieve our goals, a question often arises: Are we ready to be happy?

Many people ask me, "You have suffered so much in your life. How can you still be kind to people?" When you understand that people are often ignorant, you stop wasting time dwelling on their actions. Instead, you focus on creating a better future for yourself. They have their own world, and I have mine, and my world is great. That's what matters to me. A life without hope is worthless. As long as we have hope and faith, we have everything we need. I learned this when I was young because I struggled with hunger and poverty. During my college years, I was forced to live in a dormitory because my parents kicked me out. I had to share a room with another student. Unfortunately, the university paired me with someone who was both chaotic and unstable. We had many conflicts, and he even bought a large knife to intimidate me. I reported this to others, but no one did anything. It felt like he could hurt me at any moment and no one cared. Every night I slept uneasily while he partied and drank with other students. I never knew what night would be my last. I juggled several part-time jobs to pay for college and my room. I had no choice but to focus on my responsibilities.

Since then, I've faced many other challenges in life, and I've learned that often no one cares if you're struggling or even dying. Many people are indifferent. But if I lose hope and faith, I have nothing. Now I write for those who understand and want to learn. I ignore those who insult me and cannot appreciate what I offer with my knowledge. Some readers have been communicating with me for years, while others are rude and insinuate that I don't write my own books but get knowledge from elsewhere. I choose not to deal with these people who waste my time and patience. People are free to think what they want about me, but they know too little to draw accurate conclusions. They make assumptions based on limited knowledge of the reality in which they live. They think they know who I am just by looking at my face, and I find that incredibly foolish.

When people are ignorant, they crave attention and validation instead of working on their self-development, but that is a waste of my time. I'm not saying you shouldn't pay attention to others, but few people really deserve it. In the end, it doesn't matter what the world thinks because you will get your results anyway. For example, people can think whatever they want about me, but my life remains good; my life doesn't change because of what others, the ignorant, think.

The problem with ignorance is that it often becomes part of the personality. People see themselves in their beliefs and fear that thinking differently will change their identity. In reality, the personality they display is a constant, relative to the level of knowledge they possess. Personalities tend to manifest certain levels of consciousness, morality, and predictability. Only individuals with high levels of individuality can display a truly unique personality.

Chapter 16: The Illusion of Individuality

The personalities that people display often follow a repetitive pattern that reveals their similarities in social contexts, such as having jobs, going to the mall on weekends, getting married, and having children. Even their food choices rarely deviate from what they see others consuming. These behaviors are largely determined by their environment, and they know very little beyond it. Therefore, an independent personality can confuse them and is often perceived as insane.

When someone exhibits a higher level of consciousness, morality, and discipline, they adhere to a higher ethical standard that is less constrained by societal norms and dictates. This puts the individual at odds with the rest of the population who do not understand them and are determined to maintain their illusions of what is right and wrong. Thus, based on what identifies and differentiates people, we can derive a set of beliefs for the majority of the population because they are consistent with what is considered "right" and the idea of what "good people do".

The word "thank you" or the recognition of certain socially accepted behaviors is one such example. It doesn't matter who you are or how many people you have helped; if you refuse to say "thank you" for something that has been offered to you, or to show any kind of admiration or interest in others, they will resent you. I often observe this because most people don't impress me. They all think they are special, but their lives are not. In fact, they're very predictable, so I rarely show the enthusiasm they expect from others. But the simple fact that I don't show admiration often leads to disinterest and even hostility.

When Dale Carnegie wrote "How to Win Friends and Influence People," he described countless ways to get a message across: Make others feel special, even if they're not. People want to see their egos reinforced and reflected positively. They enjoy the illusion they live in and want to believe their lives matter, even when they do not. The vast majority of the population is forgotten after death, leaving little to be remembered. Even among the most esteemed writers, few produce works that remain relevant after a few decades. Yet many people live under the illusion of their own importance. Yet this phenomenon has probably always existed, as evidenced by the earnest expressions of men and women captured in photographs or films from decades past.

This particular form of ignorance - the belief that one is special - is prevalent in society and often hinders personal growth. After all, why would someone who believes they are special feel the need to change? So we can say that belief in one's personality, along with arrogance and a sense of social importance, characterizes those who struggle to adapt to the necessary changes of the world and to evolve. But at the extreme end of this fixation on personality is extreme poverty and death.

While individuals cannot be held accountable for their circumstances in their early years, once they reach adulthood, the outcomes of their lives are largely determined by their choices, whether conditioned or not. This truth is often unwelcome and may even be perceived as an insult. However, there are three main reasons why a person may not achieve wealth:

1. Laziness: A lack of persistence in pursuing a project over a sufficient period of time, or a tendency to seek "quick and easy" solutions.

2. Ignorance: Attempting to make money by any means necessary, including selling items that people do not want, have no value, or are completely useless to most people.

3. Stubbornness: Refusing to change or adapt to environments, demands, and situations that are in constant flux.

Every person who has asked me how to get rich and failed to do so has demonstrated laziness, ignorance, and stubbornness. Conversely, those who have successfully achieved it have worked hard, acquired the necessary knowledge, and adjusted their perspective on the world. Those who have never asked me about wealth often perceive me as lazy, ignorant, and stubborn because they are unwilling to face their own shortcomings. The truth can be offensive, especially to those who prefer to live in denial.

A recurring theme I have observed among those who complain about various life circumstances is their reluctance to acknowledge that they are responsible for creating and maintaining these situations, at least through ignorance. They observe reality within a small spectrum of understanding and resist being told that they are the source of their problems. Many people, especially in more impoverished nations, derive higher meanings for less understood realities by oversimplifying them. This is why they use the word "foreigner" to describe anyone from any part of the world, literally comparing Africans to Asians and Americans. The same goes for Americans and Europeans who think that anyone with brown skin must be an Arab. Because people are so incredibly resistant to adapting and learning, they fabricate stories for themselves about why the world is the way it is. This gives their lives meaning, even though they have to invent most of it.

Chapter 17: The Dual Nature of Ignorance

Over the years, I've watched my family, in their ignorance, make up numerous stories about my life, none of which are true or supported by evidence. However, when people lack intelligence, they ignore evidence altogether. I've identified two types of ignorance in the world: the ignorance of the uneducated and the ignorance of the educated. The uneducated are content with their unfounded assumptions and lies, creating narratives from small fragments of reality, such as inferring my lifestyle from the three months I spent in Serbia. Conversely, the educated are able to rationalize complex falsehoods using similar patterns. Both groups are ignorant, but each in its own way.

For example, I've found that college professors often display an astonishing level of ignorance despite their expertise in explanation. They can talk for hours about nothing of substance, with no significant differences in methods or results. The uneducated, on the other hand, cannot distinguish what is valuable from what is not, which is why my colleagues thought I was stupid for skipping classes in both high school and college. No one could understand how I always got high grades despite the difficulty of the exams. It's not difficult, given the predictability of the ignorant, who always follow the same patterns.

In both cases, the problems people invent, regardless of their level of education, give them a false sense of importance, which they use to build their self-image. That's why they like to gossip about me; their lives are so monotonous that there's more to say about me. When people have nothing interesting going on in their lives, they often get into a state where they think they can create meaning for themselves by choosing someone to gossip about. Having someone to gossip about gives them a delusional sense of importance and intelligence. Therefore, the more you achieve in life, the less contact you should have with such people. They drain your energy by creating problems with their gossip and spreading lies.

This behavior is often used against popular people, which is why I had to stop teaching. Instead of discussing what they learn, people focus on your personal life, because ignorant people do not learn anything; they just seek entertainment. That's why they're so ignorant. Ignorant people like to be entertained. The wise, on the other hand, read and don't ask about things that don't interfere with their own progress. The validation of the wise is self-made, not constructed through lies, slander, and gossip.

The downside of seeking validation through rumor and gossip is that people become so involved in other people's lives that they neglect their own. When they finally decide to break away from the group that validates them, those same people discourage them or leave their lives. If people you've known for years don't want or expect you to change, they will resist your growth and oppose anyone who might help you. It won't be long before they resort to nonsensical arguments, confrontation, and eventually disappear. These situations are so predictable that they can be anticipated. It's like watching someone with a mental illness concoct explanations for their condition, because this behavior is common in the general population.

With few exceptions, the vast majority of people construct a self-created world that they perceive as solid, and when something disrupts that world, they refuse to accept the change. Instead, they fabricate unproven explanations to maintain their illusions. Most people have opinions and explanations about everything, but they know very little. Their lives are dictated by habit. They rarely read, and when they do, it's often material filled with common sense popularized by those who seek to bolster their own egos. When they do pursue higher education, they seek only that which supports their arguments, not that which challenges them. This is especially true of professors who can speak at length about subjects they don't fully understand. It's common in the social sciences, where theories abound but results are often lacking.

People often lack the interest to seek out valuable information, and the intellectual capacity and humility to discern what is truly valuable. Most people do not even know how to think critically. Their thoughts are predetermined by the constants they observe in the world and what they filter through their own delusional minds.

Chapter 18: The Illusion of Conformity

Conformity does not offend or disturb anyone because it lacks truth; it is based on validating illusions and social agreements. It does not matter how many people you listen to, how many thousands of pages of books you read, or how much you think you know. Whenever you adhere to social conformity, you will never progress beyond what is permitted by society and its standards of belief. Laziness, stubbornness, and ignorance can remain hidden as long as a person stays within predictable social norms.

This state of being is a form of numbness and spiritual slavery that many have willingly accepted and become accustomed to due to their low nature and negative spiritual predisposition. It is only when one encounters someone outside of these norms that one begins to recognize these traits. For example, it is common for people to feel a sense of ignorance when speaking with me, primarily because I do not adhere to societal norms. Instead, I follow principles that transcend society itself. Time and again, I have observed that this approach confuses people as they constantly try to fit my words into their societal framework. They struggle to perceive my statements as truths or immutable laws. This refusal to acknowledge my perspective stems from their ego, which leads them to blame me for the resulting conflict of values within themselves - essentially their own cognitive dissonance - rather than recognizing their limitations.

No one enjoys the realization that most people are ineffective and useless beyond the social framework. Even if one in five thousand is considered valuable, this does little to change the broader social landscape. Those who are truly valuable often mistakenly believe in their usefulness due to the overwhelming influence of the majority mindset. However, there is a pervasive hostility to difference that causes even critical thinkers to feel isolated and ultimately conform to the views of the majority. This pressure is a constant presence in every interaction, no matter where you are on Earth.

When you try to escape these principles to avoid discomfort, you are actually fleeing from the truth. No matter how well thought out your theories or plans may be, they will not succeed without acknowledging these underlying principles. Those who think they can devise a plan to circumvent these societal realities are misguided; they are merely trying to navigate a socially imposed situation without challenging the society that created it. This phenomenon is particularly evident when I encounter so-called nomads, freelancers, and online workers. These individuals often speak as if they own important companies and are more important than others. I find their stories fascinating because there is nothing inherently special about them, and what they say about themselves is often a complete lie.

Everyone I have met in these fields has taken a job without a formal contract, working independently rather than in a traditional office setting. The only thing that distinguishes them from other workers is their precarious employment situation, which forces them to constantly seek new opportunities. They are freelancers or self-employed, but this status does not confer any special meaning. These individuals are simply responding to the global shortage of jobs, but they have not solved the underlying problem. Instead, they have inadvertently made it easier for companies to pay lower wages and fire workers with impunity.

Online workers have not initiated meaningful change; they have simply adapted to the existing challenges of employability and the constant inflation of the market. They fail to recognize that their income and freedom are limited by competition and customer loyalty. The countries they present as symbols of wealth and status are often the most impoverished in the world, because it is easier to feel richer when the average salary of the poor is low. This is why they talk about Colombia, Indonesia and Thailand as if they had chosen them, rather than acknowledging that they were allowed to enter and stay in these countries, often under very precarious conditions.

Over time, the serious consequences of an inability to accept change can lead to dire outcomes, including death. For this reason, many people disappear over time, either becoming poorer, dying of disease, or committing suicide. This is to be expected of people who cannot change harmful, unsafe, and lazy habits, whether they are addictions, unwillingness to improve, or unhealthy eating patterns. For example, those who smoke excessively demonstrate a profound disregard for their bodies and appear to be ignorant conformists. They seek to alleviate their dissatisfaction with life not through change, but through chemicals that prolong their current state. I have also met many people who appear happy on the surface, but privately confide in me that they struggle with depression and suicidal tendencies.

Chapter 19: Transcending Materialism

When we see the end of the physical body as just another phase of evolution, we can understand that consciousness is not limited by the material world with which it interacts. Instead, materialism forces consciousness to undergo constant transformation. All knowledge is created by making the unconscious conscious. But when that consciousness is dulled by chemicals, people sink deeper into their habits and unconsciousness, becoming increasingly resistant to change. Their lives become governed by pleasure rather than consciousness.

Many of these people have the ability to rationalize complex issues, but when asked to change a negative behavior, they often deflect the conversation and exhibit a strong aversion to change. Since not everyone can be admitted to a spiritual rehab center to address their struggles with life, they reside on the only known natural spiritual hospital - planet Earth. This planet serves as a refuge for souls in the universe who are unable to evolve with other races and require a higher-density reality characterized by pain, inertia and suffering resulting from ignorance. Consequently, the society we inhabit reflects this collective social mass.

The values accepted by society are reflected in the educational system, popular literature, and public discourse. Almost all of these elements reflect the same dominant paradigm. The only way to escape this paradigm is through pragmatism and confrontation with strongly held norms and beliefs. All learning is an illusion unless it becomes pragmatic. This pragmatism comes from personal perception because there is no other way to get it through a mass of delusional souls. This is why the best books are often beyond the comprehension of the greatest conformists and are hard to find.

Individuals who initiate change are often met with hostility by the conformists, who see them as a diabolical threat because of their fear of change. As a result, the vast majority of people do not learn what they should learn, but what they can learn. This is evident today as many companies refuse to publish my books and in many cases hide them from the public. As a result, when someone searches for the topics explained here, they are led to read other literature - nonsense that perpetuates illusions instead of challenging them.

Even more extraordinary is when people criticize literature that challenges their beliefs because they are unable to see their limitations. They insult and blame the author for not providing a theory that better fits their delusional beliefs and falsehoods. In fact, they often prefer liars who can provide convincing arguments to keep them exactly as they are and prevent any change. Both fiction and popular nonfiction books reveal such patterns. You can learn a great deal about society by studying these books, although they will rarely help you succeed and in many cases may drive you crazy.

The same is true of religion, which must conform to the expectations and emotional needs of the masses. This is why popular groups, such as Christians, often have a tremendous amount of fantasy in their stories. People only accept ideas that resonate with them on an emotional level. Without awareness of their inner spiritual needs, no external learning can change the structure of the mind's consciousness. This lack of awareness is why many people suffer from problems they refuse to face. The extensive use of psychotropic drugs, along with the obsession with religion, reflects a widespread flight from reality among the population. This flight does not change their spiritual state in any meaningful way. Many spirits seem to inhabit the earth as if it were an asylum for mentally disturbed souls. Drug use or adherence to a religion that merely validates common spiritual struggles only serves to mask the underlying problems.

Moreover, psychiatrists and priests often inadvertently hinder the evolution of souls and prevent them from transcending to what many call paradise by offering services that cater to emotional needs. Thus, psychiatry and religion can become significant barriers to spiritual growth by attacking the independent manifestations of the soul and reinforcing the illusion that such individuals reflect the satisfaction of various needs such as belonging, acceptance, respect, and esteem. Most people join religious groups because the teachings give meaning to their lives and foster friendships. However, they often fail to grasp how these beliefs can be experienced outside their group. They perceive the schizophrenia of the world as different from the manifestations of their own group. Similarly, those addicted to psychotropic drugs often believe that the world as it is represents the totality of existence and think that only through chemicals can life be enjoyed normally.

Chapter 20: The Illusion of Education

Since the mind only accepts what it is ready to receive, inner needs are closely tied to self-knowledge. One must rise above one's present state before one can experience thoughts of a new nature and new dreams fueled by fresh ideas and visions. Unfortunately, many people exist in a zombie-like state, governed by latent subconscious influences - whether from phrases they've heard since birth, values they've absorbed from parents, or those they've copied from friends, even those they haven't seen in years. They live according to a set of values imposed by various social structures. In many cases, these values are enforced through trauma and fear, whether through punishment, ridicule, or other emotionally distressing experiences, including those we consider normal, such as being tested in school.

If you watch the expressions on students' faces before an exam, and then watch those who fail, the answer becomes clear: for many, the outcome of an exam reflects their value to society and shapes their self-image for life. But many entrepreneurs were bad students because they cared less about their grades. When they start a new business, they pay little attention to mistakes, which allows them to learn, correct, and evolve faster than the average person who cannot think outside the box. In fact, it is much harder to teach a college student to prepare for an exam than it is to teach a child, because the college student often doesn't care about understanding; they have spent their whole lives learning how to memorize information they don't understand.

This is especially problematic when we realize that many people we trust in society, such as doctors, dentists, and nurses, don't really know what they're doing. The answer they always give me is, "That's what they told me in college," which proves that they don't care about the implications of what they teach. Even when we analyze the way people are selected for a job, we find that it is a traumatic experience in itself. Many people are so afraid of being judged that they are more determined to be accepted than to find their own way. They eventually lose the ability to dream because their self-esteem has been shaped by too many negative experiences of failure and rejection.

Furthermore, when they see no immediate rewards or encounter challenges in any area of life - from relationships to business endeavors - they are quick to give up. The average person is too weak to compromise their emotions for something greater than their social image, such as self-respect. In fact, many people will trade self-respect for anything that offers a higher income and a more socially rewarding life. That's why there is no direct correlation between school grades, failure to find a job, and success in life. For example, Jack Ma, the founder of Alibaba, was rejected by many employers before starting his company, including jobs flipping burgers. This proves that a great entrepreneur and a wealthy individual are characterized by their habits and mindset, not by society's judgments.

On the other hand, it is also true that the best entrepreneurs do not always make good employees, precisely because they are too creative and get bored easily. I didn't realize this as a child, but the reason I was always distracted and daydreaming in the classroom was because I was smarter than everyone else, not less intelligent. I was not destined to fail and end up in a middle-wage job, as the school psychologist suggested, nor was I destined to drop out of college, as my family members and professors urged me to do. Instead, I was destined to become who I am today, only I had to discover it on my own because no one would tell me.

Over time, I have discovered that the most important skills - such as creativity and the ability to think independently - although often rejected as undesirable by society at large, make us more than anyone else. Even the fact that I was always writing books as a teacher led my colleagues to perceive me as a madman writing nonsense and wasting time, rather than someone who was making a serious investment in knowledge that would take me to new heights.

Another reason people will never see your efforts is that they are determined to keep their lives as they are, rather than start over somewhere else and do something different. As a result, they cannot imagine this in others. It is precisely this inability to adapt and learn from mistakes that makes most people, especially college professors, less useful in the ever-evolving business landscape, which can contribute to the failure of many businesses. Not surprisingly, they often use outdated materials and books, condemning their students to adapt to a world that no longer exists. This is why so many graduates end up unemployed and, in some cases, homeless, despite having a college degree.

Chapter 21: The Challenge of Adapting to a Changing World

As I have often observed, most people have difficulty adapting to different contexts. They mistakenly believe that their intelligence lies in their ability to repeat tasks. However, this repetition ultimately leads to the obsolescence of organizations and institutions over time. When an organization tries to implement change, employees often resist in various ways. For example, when I was asked to teach other college professors how to improve their teaching methods, some made up excuses to avoid attending, while others distracted themselves with their cell phones, acting just like their own students.

As time goes on, the inadequacy of individuals in the world becomes more apparent as they fail to develop the necessary skills to justify their positions. While many professors can hide behind a facade of competence that they do not truly possess - largely because universities value diplomas over life experience - students face a grim reality. After the age of 30, a person is either validated by a significant career or risks lifelong unemployment, as companies typically prefer to hire recent graduates.

In recent years, with the advent of artificial intelligence, this phenomenon is accelerating; even recent graduates may soon find themselves obsolete. The only professions likely to survive in the near future are those whose skills cannot be replicated by AI, namely the arts and creativity. In other words, those who cannot think critically will find themselves increasingly marginalized. Thinking is fundamentally the art of articulating different points of view rather than simply labeling them as right or wrong. Ironically, this means that people who are perfectly indoctrinated by government institutions are often the very people that companies do not want to hire.

Many people mistakenly believe that a new government can solve problems that are rooted in a culture of misinformed and misguided individuals. Many professors waste taxpayer money by replicating the existing system rather than changing it. This misconception about unemployment arises because people do not understand that efficiency comes from change and adaptation, not from stagnation and repetition of outdated patterns. Many who consider themselves experienced and experts in their fields fail to secure employment because they feel ill-suited to a society that has moved on without them. They do not realize that the society they once knew no longer wants them precisely because they are predictable. Society must evolve through differentiation, not through mere repetition of the past.

An individual who is a polymath, though rejected by the educational system, has a higher potential for employment than someone who has spent years studying only one subject. Furthermore, as consciousness expands and deepens, the transformations in an individual's reality become more profound, leading to a greater willingness to learn and an increased capacity for understanding. Thus, the cycle of transformation is inextricably linked to the cycle of meaningful learning.

The faster society changes, the faster we must adapt if we want to improve our lives. No one works harder than the person whose efforts are changing the world. You will never outperform the best at collecting data, consulting, investing, and entrepreneurship; therefore, you will never work too much, although you can always work too little. An effective person is one who can adapt to many contexts.

When we talk about "meaningful learning," we mean knowledge that enables us to understand the world around us from multiple perspectives. The habit of accumulating meaningful knowledge reshapes our thinking and fills the void created by unmet needs in our education. Although knowledge does not provide us with physical possessions, it teaches us how to acquire them, resulting in external transformations that subsequently alter our internal structures. The more we know, the more we can do for ourselves and others, resulting in greater value that can be exchanged for wealth.

We have moved from bartering vegetables and livestock to bartering skills and knowledge. However, a significant portion of the population remains stuck in a medieval mindset. They fail to recognize the importance of cultivating their intellect for the fruits that can be exchanged, insisting instead on selling empty land when applying for jobs. They believe they deserve a good life based solely on their personality, which is the biggest lie narcissists tell themselves.

Many people fail to see the connection between what they know and what they can get, and are surprised by a world that gives them back exactly what they give - nothing. In fact, these same individuals often fail again when they are emotionally motivated to seek validation and wealth in areas where they lack knowledge. This immature and misguided thinking manifests itself every time someone asks me how I sell books, which is often. They never consider how to write a book that is worth reading; I have yet to meet anyone who has asked that question. Instead, they often go in the opposite direction, asking me how to overcome writer's block, a euphemism for having nothing meaningful to say or share. Some people even get angry when I suggest that in order to write better books they should read more. This shows how delusional they are about their own abilities. I wish them nothing but failure, lack of sales, and unemployment, as their contributions only serve to make the world worse.

Chapter 22: The Quest for True Knowledge

The illusion perpetuated by government educational institutions leads to the accumulation of countless pieces of information that are ultimately useless to the mind and do not foster a sense of freedom or accomplishment. As a result, an overabundance of information can diminish the pursuit of truth and cause individuals to cling to relativism and nihilism. Many students have expressed to me that the overwhelming amount of information they cannot use leaves them unable to find higher meanings in life. When our learning or choices are driven by external rather than internal needs, true evolution is stifled. Such learning is motivated not by pleasure but by duty, causing individuals to lose their sense of self in the process.

The problem with these distortions is that they interfere with our ability to survive. However, when you take the initiative to develop your own skills, society often invalidates those efforts. For example, because I did not formally study literature, music, or computer science, many people I meet around the world are offended by my ability to effortlessly write books, sell music, and create online businesses and applications. They perceive my accomplishments as shortcuts and cheating in life, and view my lack of formal education as somehow illegal or dishonest.

Most people interpret reality through this narrow lens because they cannot fathom a world beyond the standards they have been taught. This leads them to view alternative paths as illegitimate. They have difficulty conceptualizing individuals who are more successful and capable than themselves. In fact, many are angry at the ability of some to surpass them in accomplishments using better techniques and knowledge than what they want to believe is true.

I have been invited to dinner by many who wanted to ask questions and challenge my answers, leaving me wondering if I was wasting my time. People often seem too entrenched in their beliefs to learn anything beyond what they have convinced themselves is true. Their failures in life stem not only from a lack of luck, but also from a lack of intelligence and reason. Overall, it could be said that they are too limited in their thinking to thrive.

Many individuals are incredibly constrained by societal rules and collectively accepted knowledge, leading them to reject anyone who opposes their views and perceive them as a threat to their existence. As a group, they contribute to the avoidance of what is of value and the disappearance of important insights from the world. Such individuals rarely seek out books that present ideas they cannot share with others or that might invite criticism, living like caged animals who have accepted their condition. They also reject any idea that might invalidate their view of life.

This behavior is animalistic, indicating that these individuals are attached to their primitive survival needs through emotional attachments and tribal validation. They are not spiritual; if they claim any form of religion, it is merely a superficial attempt to validate their ignorance through an external force, often fabricated by their imagination and supported by disorganized and mistranslated pieces of information they have encountered. They will change their religion if one does not satisfy their needs, declaring the new belief to be more true than the previous one. Such individuals have not yet awakened their souls to the pursuit of knowledge.

This begs the question of whether their situation is truly unhappy or simply a consequence of their inability to adapt as the world around them evolves. The true spiritual journey begins only when a person chooses to seek answers to their problems. This journey begins in the mind and requires the spiritual maturity to recognize one's limitations - something many parents unfortunately fail to foster in their children when they overprotect them and tell them they deserve everything they want. Such parents handicap their children for life by making them too unaware of their own incompetence and maladjustment as adults.

It could also be argued that ego-driven educators, in their attachment to the system they represent, contribute to the existence of frustrated, apathetic, unhappy, and lost citizens, ensnared by the illusions of materialism and devoid of ambition for knowledge. Yet these educators are also products of the very system they perpetuate, chosen precisely for their high capacity to maintain the old system and pass it on to the next generations who yearn for better sources and methods. In fact, this is what education experts learn in college: various ways to maintain the status quo while convincing students that they are learning when they instinctively know they are not. The various educational disorders that continue to be invented are symptoms of a dysfunctional society that is so immature and irresponsible that it prefers to pass the responsibility for the future on to the children.

Chapter 23: The Manipulation of Emotions

We often observe a sense of satisfaction when a student finally grasps a subject that has eluded him. However, this satisfaction does not reflect true awareness or true evolution. Instead, it has been redirected to the educational system itself, which manipulates thought through emotion. This joy of learning manifests physically as a release from the problems associated with incomprehension-problems that the system has instilled to steer the student in a certain direction. In essence, the student who understands feels the joy of escaping the ignorance imposed by the educational system. It is similar to feeling relieved that an enemy has become a friend, when in fact the unhappiness of the original situation gave meaning to the happiness of the latter.

A similar phenomenon occurred during the coronavirus pandemic, when people felt happy after receiving their vaccinations. This happiness was conditioned by the pervasive fear of infection, which was perpetuated daily by the media. In other words, individuals were conditioned to respond in a certain way by the daily manipulation of their emotions.

Although illusions manifest in the ego through various meanings, they do not gain significance from the meanings we assign to them. Instead, they remain illusions because true awareness lies in recognizing that we can only determine our own meanings by what moves us forward, rather than by conforming to the herd mentality of society. The most challenging yet powerful realization in life is that most people, with very few exceptions, are not truly alive. They exist in a state between the memories of yesterday and the obligations of tomorrow. Lacking an understanding of the meaning of life, they remain blind to possibilities beyond their limited perspective. This narrow view shapes their identity, their behavior, and the narratives they tell themselves and others to justify their actions. The more ignorant they feel, the more important they believe themselves to be. Their sense of importance is reinforced by the ignorance of others. They think that if a large number of people validate the falsehoods they cling to, it somehow increases their importance.

This need to belong to a majority makes people susceptible to manipulation, and it is from this dynamic that pride arises. For example, during the coronavirus pandemic, many found satisfaction in being part of the majority that received the vaccine. This feeling would have been diminished if they had been in the minority that refused it, but in both cases they were relying solely on the suggestions of authoritative figures who throughout history have lied and harmed their own people for socialist ideals. In fact, Agenda 21, a blueprint for sustainable development signed by

178 governments, discusses the importance of health care and vaccines as part of a broader strategy to reduce poverty and combat overpopulation. The document systematically links health services to sustainable development. But how can these two issues be linked if we really want people to be healthier and live longer?

Labeling those who can observe the obvious as lunatics or conspiracy theorists does not invalidate the illogical assumption that more health care will solve the problems of overpopulation and poverty - unless we deliberately avoid discussing slow genocide through health care programs. One would have to be incredibly naive not to see this, but most people are, which is why such documents are ignored by the vast majority, proving that civilization has learned nothing from historical and similarly gullible mistakes. The majority is so determined not to be perceived as ignorant that they end up doing exactly what an ignorant person does: ignoring logic.

Reflecting on my own experiences as a student, I remember being kicked out of class for refusing to follow certain rules or simply for laughing too much. My laughter seemed to offend many teachers who believed that the classroom should be a place of suffering. My classmates often saw me leave the room smiling and acted as if I had committed a crime. They recognized that I was merely resisting unfair rules or expressing joy, but they perceived me as wrong, not themselves. Later, when they received their exam results, they saw those papers as definitive representations of their potential, allowing the educational system to dictate their future.

As a teacher, I experienced a similar situation. My students often laughed at my jokes, leading some to believe that my classes lacked the seriousness of others. Yet the students were consistently exceptional-quick, capable, and highly motivated. Unlike many college graduates who felt unmotivated in life, my students traveled extensively, pursued further studies, and remained eager to learn more about the world. They won numerous awards and secured the best jobs because their minds were awakened and ready for the necessary journey ahead.

Chapter 24: Breaking Free of Illusion

The whirlwind of illusion keeps the spiritual being entangled in the lies constructed by its own mind. This entanglement can last a lifetime and extend across lifetimes, binding the individual into karmic cycles and preventing them from realizing their ability to create their own destiny. When this potential is nurtured, fear often drives the individual to seek familiarity rather than change. In times of fear, people cling more tightly to what they have. The answer lies in embracing change and starting over, but many fail to see this, leading to a lack of understanding of their life's challenges.

In addition, when life is comfortable, people often resist the discomfort that change brings. They reject any opportunity to escape the cycles in which they find themselves. It is often through sickness and death that these cycles are broken, usually permanently. The new beginnings that should occur in life often manifest later through rebirth. An individual may find themselves in a new context - different family, nationality, and circumstances - and be forced to relearn the lessons they previously resisted.

For example, someone who wanted to travel to India but feared communication barriers or loneliness might be reborn in India and experience both her desires and her fears. Similarly, a person who clung to wealth and lived in a castle surrounded by servants may be reborn in poverty and learn to earn the help of others not through money but through their personality. However, this does not guarantee that individuals will learn the lessons they are meant to. Most simply observe their unpleasant experiences and conclude that what they have is all they can attain, never venturing into anything new or different. Many have never traveled to another city in their own country, and few know all the cities in their nation or neighboring countries. Some even believe that travel requires wealth, which is a misconception.

While freedom requires some financial resources, it does not require a fortune. The cost of human life is relatively low; a person with as little as $5,000 a month can travel anywhere in the world and live like a local. Although $5,000 may seem substantial, it seems so primarily because most people in the world do not have access to such resources. For someone born 50 years ago, when the cost of living was lower, this amount would seem even more significant. In today's world, being a millionaire has become so commonplace that it is hardly noticed. The new aspiration is to become a billionaire, and in the future it will probably be the trillionaires who capture the spotlight. This shift in focus is largely due to the diminishing value of money over time, caused by general inflation.

Life becomes harder for the majority who find themselves ill-equipped for a world that is falling behind, while those who have embraced hardship and innovation embark on journeys to greater wealth and freedom. I am certainly reaping the rewards of many years of hard work while watching family members who never helped me out of selfishness die in misery and many friends go nowhere in life despite their college degrees. Even my students, who didn't take me seriously when I taught them important lessons about life, now claim to want the same life I have because they feel trapped in a life they wanted despite my warnings that it was not the best option.

In a global economy, the methods of creating wealth are more relative, and we can no longer use the methods by which our ancestors prospered. In fact, it is foolish to believe and wait for a government to make changes instead of seeking those changes ourselves through migration. For example, starting a business in Europe may require considerable effort, while the same venture may be relatively easy in another part of the world. This disparity stems from the different structures that facilitate or impede access to wealth in different regions.

In Europe, access to wealth has historically been restricted to prevent the lower classes from competing with the upper classes. Conversely, in the United States, competition is a fundamental aspect of the nation's prosperity. The growth of the United States stagnated when the upper classes attempted to block access to wealth for the lower classes. This struggle is why social issues such as racism and discrimination are so sensitive in the U.S. The nation's very identity is at stake, and until that identity embraces diversity, the country may face a bleak future. We grow through diversity and innovation, and the United States, Canada,

Singapore, Switzerland, and Australia are good examples. They falter only when they forget this fundamental truth.

Chapter 25: The Power of Imagination

The greatest fear of many is the fear of having nothing. However, there is a unique blessing in having no attachments - nothing to fear losing - and the ability to start over. The wisest people in history, from various monks to the greatest Greek philosophers, sought to possess little because they understood this profound truth. They recognized that light is governed by darkness, or, as the Hindu scriptures suggest, the visible emerges from the invisible-the atom exists within the molecule, which is influenced by the conscious mind. For the mind to awaken to its potential to change reality, it must first be free. Only when the mind feels free can it recognize and act upon its potential. This freedom comes from self-awareness and an understanding of the laws of the universe.

To those who do not understand these laws, wealth and poverty may appear to be opposite states of existence, each offering a different way of experiencing reality. However, this distinction only makes sense if we view money as a means to an end. When we look at this distinction through the lens of opportunity and our relationship to the physical world and those who participate in it, we see that it manifests in ways far beyond what the physical world presents. A person can lend us the money we need, a bank can make a loan, and we can generate ideas that are valuable and recognized by society that allow us to acquire that money.

Through our ideas and our ability to observe reality factually, we can achieve goals that once seemed impossible, at least according to the social context to which we were exposed. Thus, we can say that imagination is the most powerful human ability: what you can imagine, you can achieve. In fact, it is the best way to develop neurological pathways that enhance the perception of the kind of life you want to experience. Our imaginative abilities guide the development of our brains, which then help us find possibilities. For this reason, we can assert that the mind, as the source of our imagination, has the ability to alter our intelligence and increase our potential for success.

Many athletes have discovered this and have used their imagination to mentally prepare for the goals that lie ahead. You can use the same principle to access alternate realities. If you can imagine having a conversation with your other self, who exists in an alternate reality where you are who you want to be, you can gain insights from that self that may be difficult for outsiders to understand or dismiss as mere fantasy. This metacognitive ability allows you to perceive things that may have previously remained outside your spectrum of self-knowledge. Furthermore, when the imagination provides the answers we seek, it becomes as tangible as any other element of material reality.

Consider, for example, that before you make a decision, you can imagine both outcomes, gaining insight from a timeline in which your future self is already experiencing what your present self has not yet seen. In this way, you can have a conversation with that future self and ask what it feels, gaining deeper insight into the immense pool of knowledge that resides in your subconscious mind. In addition, this exercise can awaken the potential to dream premonitions while you sleep, allowing you to uncover secrets that others may never reveal to you, including hidden plans against you. We often receive warnings during sleep about things we are not consciously aware of during our daily routines, allowing us to prepare for possible plots against us.

This imaginative potential expands your awareness far beyond what your imagination alone can contemplate. By using your imagination frequently and purposefully, you can uncover possibilities and better prepare yourself mentally and emotionally for the challenges ahead. When making a decision, simply ask yourself What is the worst that could happen? Am I ready for it?

Because the educational system often suppresses this ability - by devaluing the potential for art and creative expression - we must develop it as adults. We can establish a morning ritual of imagining the kind of life we want and asking the other self in a parallel reality who he is and what he has done to acquire these things. The thoughts that flow into our mind from this other world, this alternate future, will appear in real time, for there is no measurable time for the mind.

Our telepathic abilities are expressed at the very moment we formulate questions, although it may take time for us to learn to recognize the thoughts that come to us. They first manifest as energy and vibration that must be decoded through our emotions.

Telepathy isn't a word-by-word experience, but rather a decoding of symbols, meanings and feelings that we eventually turn into words in our minds. It is like seeing a door and knowing what it means without having to verbalize the word "door" before using it. In our daily lives we perform many tasks that are not verbalized. Telepathy works on the same principles when we communicate with our other expressions in parallel worlds.

Chapter 26: The Mental Prison of Education

The system that humans have built for themselves acts as a mental prison that shapes the consciousness of those educated within it. It adapts individuals to think and look alike, creating a uniformity that many do not recognize as problematic. On the contrary, people often take pride in being replicas of one another, sharing the same beliefs, experiencing similar outcomes, and going through the same dramas. They have normalized their lives, even consuming media that reflect their own experiences.

In addition, people have learned to accept the daily challenges they face and see nothing wrong with enduring them. Many have told me that life without problems is boring, indicating that they derive meaning from their struggles. This should be considered abnormal, but it is not, as those who hold these beliefs are often conditioned by the very system that perpetuates them. Change must occur within the individual before they can see the flaws in their thinking.

People become so conditioned by the system that they forget that the solutions presented are merely reflections of the problems created by that same system. For example, many complain that schools only teach them to memorize irrelevant subjects. Yet this is exactly what the system requires: people who are able to memorize information that has little value in their lives - essentially educated robots who can reproduce the world as it is without questioning or changing it. The system forces people to conform to the very reality they wish to perpetuate. The problem, then, is not education itself, but what people expect of it. Both educators and students strive to maintain a society that resists change, which leads them to prioritize memorization over critical thinking. This is what society needs to sustain itself.

Those who have numerous ideas, question excessively, and refuse to adapt to familiar realities are often deemed unfit for the system. As a result, students who struggle academically often internalize the belief that they are worthless or lacking in intelligence. This idea is a falsehood perpetuated by the educational system. Many capable students simply do not fit the mold of obedient learners; they are better suited for independence and, with the right guidance, can achieve significant financial success.

I have met numerous students who struggled within the conventional educational model, but could learn quickly if given the tools to think critically. I am one of those individuals. I was never a good student; I always viewed the school system as a waste of time and the teachers as ineffective and arrogant. But because my teaching style was different from the norm, few students saw the benefits of learning from me. Most people are so entrenched in the untruths they live that the truth feels foreign and may even seem wrong. Consequently, I stopped wasting my time teaching those who were unwilling to learn because few students recognized my value.

The assessment process within education embodies the hypocrisy of a system that forces students to grasp solutions to problems defined as relevant by that same system. It is not surprising, then, that children perceive school as an obligation and a sacrifice; anything else would feel unnatural. This method of learning disrupts the natural evolution of the mind, which ultimately has no alternative outside of this process. Any unexpected realizations that arise during the obligation of schooling, which relate to an individual's unique universe, are often unappreciated sacrifices. As a result, those who succeed and go on to college are not necessarily the best among us, but rather the most adept at enforcing the system without changing it.

The learning that the spirit requires from the outside world often manifests itself through suggestion-an unexpected coincidence in the environment that does not match a person's current situation. It could be an encounter with an unexpected person or an opportunity that seems out of reach. However, unless we cultivate childlike curiosity, we will consistently fail to recognize these opportunities as we develop our minds to achieve better results. Many fail to act because they do not see what their minds will not acknowledge. The need to act only arises when it is connected to something intrinsic to the individual.

In other words, a person will only respond if he perceives a benefit and is willing to pursue it. This is a critical point that proponents of visualization techniques often miss. They mistakenly believe that there is a direct correlation between visualization and manifestation, but for this to be true, one would have to disregard the mind, individuality, and the spirit itself in its immortal consciousness, which is illogical.

Chapter 27: Visualization and Possibility

Visualization techniques serve to link the subconscious with the conscious mind. They create conscious habits that help us identify the right opportunities in our environment and enable us to act more quickly and accurately. Affirmations work in much the same way. For example, consider someone who has been told repeatedly, "You will never be successful with that personality," or "Getting rich is not for people like us because we are poor". When the right opportunities come along, these people often miss them because they have been conditioned to consciously reject what comes their way. I have seen this phenomenon many times, and it often seems so absurd that it is hard to believe.

For example, I once offered a friend the opportunity to travel to China to develop his business, but he declined because of the distance and the fear of wasting his vacation time since he only had a few days off from work. Similarly, when I offered him books on how to build a business, he didn't even bother to read them. Yet his dream was to become a successful entrepreneur. Not surprisingly, that dream never materialized. He attracted the opportunities and aspirations he had through me, but ultimately failed because he was unwilling to sacrifice two weeks of his life and too lazy to travel to another continent. Most people are simply not mentally prepared to pursue what they say they want in life. Their actions do not match their words, which is a clear indication that they will never achieve their stated desires. Any other reasons they give to justify their inaction are just excuses to stay in their current situation.

Unlike my friend, I accepted a job offer in China that paid less than half of what I was making at a company just a five-minute walk from my home. I took the job, which was four flights away and in a very cold city, before I had the money to cover the travel expenses. An unexpected loan from the bank came days later, as no one I knew would lend me the money, despite my insistence that I would pay it back immediately from my salary. With plenty of free time as a lecturer in China, I wrote most of my books there. Just a few years later, I left that job to become a full-time writer and travel the world.

Meanwhile, the other friend remains exactly where he was 15 years ago, still working as a security guard because he failed to develop his business and struggled to find a job related to his college degree. Not long after, he became obsessed with visiting his psychiatrist and taking psychotropic drugs to cope with his miserable life. This is the definition of a loser. But he made himself the loser he became. You inevitably become what you define yourself to be by your attitudes, words and choices.

Many people believe that poverty determines their outcomes, but poverty is not a serious problem; rather, it is a financial condition that can be overcome through the pursuit of opportunity and knowledge. I have seen this repeatedly in my own life and in the lives of my followers. A person does not remain in poverty simply because they are poor; they remain in poverty because they do not seek opportunities to learn, improve, and develop the skills necessary to achieve their dream job.

In addition, many people hold the misguided belief that they must know the next step in their lives and that this next step will determine their entire existence. This assumption is both arrogant and shortsighted, as individuals often achieve much more through areas of life they never imagined. The best opportunities that people I know have found were not related to what they originally thought they could do; in many cases, they were skills they learned on their own.

The difference between these people and the average person is their willingness to learn, to try, to fail, and to learn from their mistakes. They are also open to pursuing opportunities around the world, going where the doors open. They cross continents and achieve things that locals often struggle to find. Many of my former students have secured jobs in countries where locals struggle to find work. They did this because they kept an open mind and looked for opportunities beyond their comfort zone.

Then there are those who are so determined to succeed that they will stop at nothing. One of my readers moved to England on a student visa and immediately found a job waiting tables in a restaurant. She secured this job by going door to door with copies of her resume. Once she had a job, a tiny room, and her visa, she maintained that lifestyle for as long as it took to finish college. Then she got a well-paying job in London, where she still lives.

Chapter 28: The Journey to Manifestation

The solutions to our problems are not always simple. We often have to go through several stages before we can manifest our dreams. However, this process only takes place when we are mentally prepared. Therefore, it is crucial to visualize and affirm our desired results before they materialize. This can be as simple as looking at pictures of what we want each night and then closing our eyes and imagining ourselves in those scenarios. The phrases we repeat to ourselves should contain affirmations that increase our magnetic potential to attract what we want. For example, if someone has been told for years, "You're poor and you'll never get rich," they should replace that phrase with something like, "I am poor, but I can be rich". Then they should keep repeating, "I can be rich".

You really can be rich. Everyone has that potential; you just have to recognize it within yourself and keep the momentum going toward your goal. It doesn't matter how long it takes to achieve your dreams; they are always attainable. You have to consider what needs to change in you to speed up the process. Certainly someone who reads voraciously has a much higher capacity for understanding compared to the average person who struggles to grasp their reality because they cannot see what they cannot understand.

I have consistently accelerated results in my life, even when all seemed lost and hope was absent, because I am a fast reader and I read a lot. When working 16 hours a day yielded no financial return and my life seemed bleak, I devoured everything I could learn about faith, magic and the occult. I then applied the techniques I learned, searching for the most effective methods. Though imperfect, my determination and faith in the process brought me so close to my goal that the only way to fail was to say no when the opportunity presented itself.

Since then, I have continued to overcome challenges created by others due to their discrimination, racism, envy, and other negative emotions. Meanwhile, I have observed that many people can achieve what they want, but reject the possibility because of lack of knowledge or fear. They either don't read my books after meeting me, or they are too afraid to change. I find this rather ridiculous, but people are ultimately responsible for their own destiny. Therefore, I never try to dissuade anyone from acting on their ignorance, nor do I try to convince anyone to read my books.

I have come to realize that many people are simply too blind to see the value of what is in front of them, even when it comes from an author. They laugh at what I say and assume that I cannot write extensively or have significant knowledge, but they are acting against their own best interests. What they think of me does not change my reality; it only defines them and their outcomes in life. In fact, I expect nothing from someone who insults me; they are simply being true to their nature. I would be foolish to expect an idiot to act differently than his nature dictates.

Most people are so determined to maintain their current lives, even though they claim to want to change, that it is a complete waste of time to try to help them. For example, I had a friend who was a fitness trainer and had read extensively about starting a business. She proudly showed me her extensive collection of books on developing a business in her field. While I found this impressive, it was not enough; she lacked an actual business. At the time, I owned an online sports store that was doing well, but it was taking up too much of my time and I wanted to sell it. I suggested offering it to my friend with no strings attached. To my surprise, she refused, claiming that she did not understand online business. I insisted that I could explain what she needed to know and help her transition the business into a physical one, allowing her to sell directly to her clients at the gym. Still, she rejected the offer - a free offer.

Months later, when she lost her gym job and was temporarily freelancing, I again offered her the online store, and again she declined my gift. She turned down a golden opportunity to run her own athletic apparel business with my help. So why was she reading so many business books? What was the point of all her Law of Attraction techniques if opportunities were presented to her for free and she said no? Obviously, this woman made no changes in her life and several years later she is still doing what she was doing, now working for a new gym and never developing any kind of business. It is not true that reading books is a waste of time, as some people believe, but just as action without knowledge is useless, you need both. Reading becomes a waste of time if you do not apply what you read.

Chapter 29: The Fear of Possibility

The primary reason many people lead unhappy lives is their fear of the opportunities that come their way, which stems from a lack of mental preparation. They often lack an awareness of what is possible, who they are as individuals, and what they can achieve. While some experience misfortunes that seem unique to them, others attract positive situations that elude most. For example, it may seem impossible that a bank would call you out of the blue to offer you money, but it happened to me just when I needed it. Since then, I have found myself in numerous situations where my focus has led me exactly where I wanted to be, even when the opportunities initially seemed out of reach.

Certain experiences happen to you and no one else, and there is no need to explain them logically. Many people ask me how I can write so many books so fast, but they will never understand because they are not me; they do not have what it takes. No matter what I say, they will remain ignorant. In fact, I have realized that I waste my time explaining how I write books because people listen and then distort my words or make up theories that I never mentioned.

I recall a conversation with an elderly woman in a religious group in which I explained that I was a college professor and had done various consulting jobs. I also mentioned my extensive reading and research of historical information. However, this misguided woman told the rest of the group that I had gathered my knowledge from some magical records in the air. Such experiences with adults in religious groups have caused me to lose interest in their meetings. Christians have accused me of talking to demons, while Freemasons have assumed that I was talking to the spirits of the dead. The level of ignorance in people's minds has forced me to realize that they are wasting my time because they are not listening to what I am saying. Instead, they seek confirmation of their own beliefs in my words, distort my statements, and spread false rumors based on their assumptions because they are both too arrogant and too ignorant to understand my message. Because of these experiences, I no longer feel the need to explain anything about what I do.

I allow the ignorant to remain ignorant and accept their fate, for they will always act according to their nature. In fact, all the religious groups I have encountered have proven to be a complete waste of time, filled with individuals who invent nonsense and cling to dogmas and misinterpretations. They understand nothing, not even their own texts. They are individuals walking around pretending to be important. Rosicrucianism, Christianity, Freemasonry, and many other groups, including Buddhism, are nothing more than a circus of clowns. Their level of understanding is so incredibly low that you have to be equally stupid to find anything useful in the chaos. The only positive aspect I have observed in religious groups is when individuals sit quietly in their chairs, as even their chanting can be irritating to my ears.

While you should never ignore what is presented to you, it is often the case that the things presented to you only lead you in the opposite direction. I have come to this realization through my experiences with various religious groups. Their ignorance, delusions, hypocrisy, lies, and lack of respect forced me to realize my own worth and to write more and faster. It is true that everything has a purpose, but sometimes that purpose is simply to realize your own worth. When you meet many ignorant people, you should not feel discouraged, but rather empowered. After these experiences, I moved to Albania, Greece, Malaysia, the Philippines, and Thailand, where I wrote extensively and enjoyed life on the beach. They can think whatever they want; it has no value to me. My life is fulfilling, while theirs is dictated by the delusions in their minds. In fact, two of the most foolish questions people often ask me are: "Which religion is best?" and "Which author do you recommend?" I find it amazing that these questions are even asked. These people deserve only silence.

People ask questions based on the reality they know, and if they are arrogant, they see very little, so their questions often make no sense. They often have nothing to do with reality itself, but rather with their beliefs. They get angry when I tell them the truth because they have no empathy for it. They are too determined to prove themselves right, which is foolish. If you are wrong, how will you ever know if you keep trying to find proof of your own misconceptions? Many people who can't sing, for example, should admit it and take singing lessons instead of forcing others to accept something that simply isn't there - a confirmation of a reality that doesn't exist. If one lacks talent, the best course of action is to admit it and work on self-improvement rather than trying to force a result that will never materialize. A man must first recognize his needs before he can seek, find, and accept the knowledge that will help him achieve his desires.

Chapter 30: Confronting Trauma

Many people have difficulty learning because they resist change. Change can be intimidating, causing people to cling to habits that have proven harmful in order to avoid bringing shame into their lives. For some, it takes years to recognize a series of mistakes, even when solutions are consistently presented. But what the conscience does not recognize, the eyes cannot see. For consciousness to awaken, it requires sufficient knowledge that can be accumulated through repeated experience with similar mistakes. It is through the comparative analysis of these experiences that perception evolves, allowing the individual to later recognize answers. Only then is such an answer accepted because it has been acknowledged by the individual and has become part of his understanding.

In essence, we only accept what we perceive as our own, and only what resonates with our identity feels authentic. This is why many traumas remain buried in the unconscious; we often refuse to accept events that have occurred in our lives. Denial of these memories leads us to systematically avoid experiences that might evoke similar feelings, all in an effort to escape potential imagined suffering. Consequently, individuals who refuse to face their mistakes and traumas tend to constrict their physical and mental space for fear of expansion.

This fear of change is compounded by the belief that safety can only be found in the presence of others who provide psychological reinforcement. This belief fosters a fear of isolation, which is inextricably linked to the fear of change. When we fear change, we are essentially afraid of starting over without the support and companionship of others. As a result, we emotionally limit our potential in life by conforming to what is common, known, and predictable. Yet success, fulfillment, and happiness often lie beyond these fears. Thus, the fear of loss and failure is closely related to the fear of success and happiness. In fact, the fear of unhappiness can cause people to unconsciously avoid happiness altogether. Individuals may fear becoming happy because this process carries the potential risk of experiencing unhappiness.

The more trauma a person has in their past, the more they try to block it out of their mind. The effort to forget these experiences can condition their choices in the present, leading them to avoid potential risks associated with facing similar traumas, along with the associated guilt and shame. This is a form of self-protection, albeit at the expense of personal growth, as it denies the potential to gain more from life. Ultimately, however, our memories need to be confronted until they no longer have an emotional impact, even though they may remain part of an individual's memory for a lifetime - or even several lifetimes. Only when we are able to face our fears can we finally discover the essence of who we are.

With this understanding, we can persist in realizing our potential as revealed to us through our imagination and the dreams we aspire to. Anything we wish to become is only a choice away. But it all begins with the choice to dream.

Glossary of Terms

Audacity: The ability to make decisions quickly and effectively, often in the face of uncertainty or fear. In this book, audacity refers to the courage and wisdom needed to make informed decisions that lead to success and personal growth.

Conformity: The tendency to change one's behavior or thinking to conform to the majority or societal norms. The book discusses how conformity can hinder personal growth and critical thinking, as people often prioritize fitting in over making independent decisions.

Doubt: A feeling of uncertainty or lack of conviction, often about oneself or one's abilities. Doubt is described as a poison that can hinder personal growth and decision-making, often instilled by others who claim to love or support us.

Ego: The sense of self or personal identity, often characterized by self-importance and a need for validation. The book explores how the ego can be a barrier to personal growth and true happiness, often leading people to seek external validation rather than inner wisdom.

Fear: An emotional response to perceived threat or danger that often leads to avoidance or inaction. Fear has been identified as a major obstacle to making effective decisions and achieving personal goals. Overcoming fear is a central theme of this book.

Ignorance: A lack of knowledge or awareness that often leads to misguided beliefs and actions: Ignorance is discussed as a common condition among many people that leads to poor decision making and lack of personal growth. The book emphasizes the importance of seeking knowledge and wisdom to overcome ignorance.

Karma: The spiritual principle of cause and effect in which actions and intentions affect future experiences. Karma is discussed in the context of personal growth and decision-making, emphasizing the importance of taking responsibility for one's actions and their consequences.

Perseverance: The ability to persevere or persist in the face of difficulty or delay. Perseverance is emphasized as a key trait for achieving success and overcoming obstacles. It is often paired with speed and sacrifice in the book.

Pragmatism: A practical approach to problem solving and decision making that focuses on what works rather than theoretical ideals. The book emphasizes the importance of pragmatism in learning and personal growth, as theoretical knowledge alone is not enough to make effective decisions.

Selfishness: The quality of being overly or exclusively concerned with oneself, often at the expense of others. Selfishness is discussed as a common trait that can lead to poor decision making and strained relationships. The book explores how selfish people often punish those who help them.

Spiritual Evolution: The process of personal growth and development, often involving the pursuit of wisdom and self-knowledge. Spiritual evolution is a central theme of the book, emphasizing the importance of personal growth and self-discovery in making effective decisions and achieving happiness.

Wisdom: The ability to think and act with knowledge, experience, understanding, common sense, and insight. Wisdom is highlighted as a key factor in making effective decisions and achieving personal growth. The book discusses the role of wisdom in overcoming fear and ignorance.

Zombie-like state: A metaphorical state of mind characterized by a lack of awareness, critical thinking, and personal growth. The book uses the term "zombie-like state" to describe the condition of many people who are deeply ignorant and conformist, living in a state of mental stagnation.

Book Review Request

D ear reader,

Thank you for purchasing this book! I would love to know your opinion. Writing a book review helps in understanding the readers and also impacts other readers' purchasing decisions. Your opinion matters. Please write a book review!

Your kindness is greatly appreciated!

About the Author

Dan Desmarques is a renowned author with a remarkable track record in the literary world. With an impressive portfolio of 28 Amazon bestsellers, including eight #1 bestsellers, Dan is a respected figure in the industry. Drawing on his background as a college professor of academic and creative writing, as well as his experience as a seasoned business consultant, Dan brings a unique blend of expertise to his work. His profound insights and transformational content appeal to a wide audience, covering topics as diverse as personal growth, success, spirituality, and the deeper meaning of life. Through his writing, Dan empowers readers to break free from limitations, unlock their inner potential, and embark on a journey of self-discovery and transformation. In a competitive self-help market, Dan's exceptional talent and inspiring stories make him a standout author, motivating readers to engage with his books and embark on a path of personal growth and enlightenment.

Also Written by the Author

1. 66 Days to Change Your Life: 12 Steps to Effortlessly Remove Mental Blocks, Reprogram Your Brain and Become a Money Magnet

2. A New Way of Being: How to Rewire Your Brain and Take Control of Your Life

3. Abnormal: How to Train Yourself to Think Differently and Permanently Overcome Evil Thoughts

4. Alignment: The Process of Transmutation Within the Mechanics of Life

5. Audacity: How to Make Fast and Efficient Decisions in Any Situation

6. Beyond Belief: Discovering Sacred Moments in Everyday Life

7. Beyond Illusions: Discovering Your True Nature

About the Publisher

This book was published by 22 Lions Publishing.

www.22Lions.com

www.ingramcontent.com/pod-product-compliance
Lightning Source LLC
Chambersburg PA
CBHW071248150726
48001CB00018B/461